Lives Bound Together

signed by the author

Susan Schoelwer

GEORGE WASHINGTON'S
MOUNT ★ VERNON

IN MEMORY OF
THE AFRO AMERICANS
WHO SERVED AS SLAVES
AT MOUNT VERNON
THIS MONUMENT MARKING THEIR
BURIAL GROUND
DEDICATED
SEPTEMBER 21 1983
MOUNT VERNON
LADIES ASSOCIATION

Lives Bound Together

Slavery at George Washington's Mount Vernon

Negros
Belonging to George Washington in his own right and by Marriage

G.W			Dower		
Names	**ages**	**Remarks**	**Names**	**ages**	**Remarks**
Tradesmen &c.			Tradesmen &c.		
Nat .. Smith		His wife Lucy. D.R. dow.	Tom Davis B. lay.		wife at Mr. Lears
George . D°.		Ditto . Lydia R.T. D°.	Simms .. Carp.		D°. Daphne — French's
Isaac . Carp.		...... Kitty Dairy D°.	Cyrus ... Post.		D°. Lucy R.T. ... G.W
James – D°.	40	..... Darcus M.H. G.W	Wilson .. Ditto	15	no wife
Sambo – D°.		..... Agnes R.T. dow.	Godfrey . Cart.		Wife .. Mima Mr. H. dow.
Davy – D°.		..... Edy . U.T. G.W	James – D°.		D°. ... Alla – D°. – D°.
Joe ... D°.		..... Dolshy Spin. dow.	Hanson .. Dist.		No wife ...
Tom . Coop.		..... Nanny M.H. G.W	Peter .. D°.		. Ditto .
Moses . D°.		No Wife	Nat .. D°.		Ditto.
Jacob ... D°.		. Ditto	Daniel . D°.		Ditto
George Gard.		His wife Sall . D.R. dow.	Simothy . D°.		
Harry – D°.		No wife	Ha: Joe . Ditch.		wife Lydia. D.R . G.W
Boatswain Ditc.		His wife Mustilla Spin. G.W	Chrigs .. D° L.		D°. May Wests
Dundee . D°.		His wife at Mr. Lears	Marcus .. D°.		no wife
Charles . D°.		Ditto . Fanny U.T. dow.	Lucy .. Cook		Husb°. H. Frank . G.W
Ben .. D°.		Ditto .. Peony R.T. G.W	Peggy		no . Husband
Ben .. Miller		Ditto ... Sinah Mr. H. dow.	Charlotte . Sempt.		No husband
Forester D°.		No Wife	Sall .. H. W.		D°.
Nathan Cook	31	Wt. .. Peg. M.H. G.W	Caroline .. D°.		Husb°. Peter Hardman
W. Muclus B. lay.		D°. .. Capt. Marshalls	Fitty .. Mill.		D°. Isaac Carp. G.W
Juba . Carter		No wife	Alce .. Spin.		Charles Freeman
Matilda Spinner		Boson .. Ditcher	Betty Davis. D°.		Mr. Washington's Dick
Frank H. Serv.		Wife . Lucy – Cook	Dolshy		Husb°. Joe Carp. G.W
Will ... Shoem.		Jama – no wife	Anna		D°. lives at George Town
			Lady	21	No Husband
			Delphy		Ditto . D°.
			Peter Cam. Fente.		No wife
			Alla ... D°.		Husb°. James Cart. dow.
Amount	24		Amount	28	
Mansion House			Mansion House		
Payed Labour			Will		wife aggy D.R. G.W
Frank ...	80	No Wife	Joe . Postil.		D°. Sall. R.T. D°.
Gunner ...	90	Wife . Judy . R.T. G.W	Mike		No wife - son to Lucy
Jam . Cook	60	Ditto . Alce M.H. D°.	Sinah		Husb°. Miller Ben. G.W
			Mima		D°. Godfrey Wag. dow.
			Lucy		No Husband
			Grace		Husb°. Mr. Lears - Juba
			Letty		No husband
			Nancy		Ditto - D°
			Winer		Ditto - D°
			Eve	17	Ditto - a dwarf
			Delia	14	Ditto - her sister
			Children		
			Phil		Son to Lucy
Amount ..	3		Patty		Daughter to D°

Lives Bound Together

Slavery at George Washington's Mount Vernon

Introduction by *Annette Gordon-Reed*

Biographies by *Jessie MacLeod*

Essays by
Mary V. Thompson
Philip D. Morgan
Molly H. Kerr
Eleanor Breen
Esther C. White
Scott E. Casper
Maurie D. McInnis
Rohulamin Quander
Gloria Tancil Holmes
ZSun-nee Matema

Susan P. Schoelwer, Editor

Mount Vernon Ladies' Association

Publication of
Lives Bound Together:
Slavery at George Washington's Mount Vernon
and the exhibition's associated scholarly conference
generously provided by

Nimick Forbesway Foundation

Exhibition funding generously provided by

Ambassador and Mrs. Nicholas F. Taubman

Dr. Scholl Foundation
An Anonymous Donor

Maribeth and Wm. Harold Borthwick
The Challenge Foundation
Mr. Paul Neely
David Bruce Smith Fund
Catherine M. and Frederick H. Waddell
The Honorable and Mrs. Togo D. West, Jr.

Contents

Foreword

As the 21st Regent of the Mount Vernon Ladies' Association, which has owned and operated George Washington's Mount Vernon since 1860, it is my privilege to present to the public *Lives Bound Together: Slavery at George Washington's Mount Vernon*. Together, this publication and the exhibition that it accompanies mark an important step in the Association's continuing commitment to preserve and present Washington's home as closely as possible to its appearance during his lifetime. That commitment stems directly from the mandate articulated by our founder, Ann Pamela Cunningham: "Those who go to the Home in which he lived and died, wish to see in what he lived and died!"

The vast majority of Mount Vernon's more than one million annual visitors are drawn to the estate by their interest in the towering figure of George Washington, America's preeminent founding father. Washington has long been justly renowned as our nation's "indispensable man" for his pivotal roles as commander in chief of the Continental Army, president of the Constitutional Convention, and first president of the United States of America. Many visitors are also interested in knowing more about the enslaved people of Mount Vernon, who made up more than 90% of the plantation's population at the time of George Washington's death in 1799.

As the title suggests, *Lives Bound Together* addresses two distinct, but interconnected, perspectives on slavery at Mount Vernon, on the one hand tracing Washington's evolving ideas on the issue, culminating in his decision to grant freedom (by the terms of his will) to the slaves that he owned, and, on the other, exploring the experiences of those whose lives were spent in bondage. Although Mount Vernon's eighteenth-century slaves left no written accounts, rich evidence of their experiences survives in the form of archaeological findings, plantation buildings, and landscape features, and in Washington's extensive writings—his letters and diaries, ledgers, account books, and detailed reports compiled by his farm and plantation managers. Indeed, it might be said that through his meticulous recordkeeping, Washington wrote the biographies of the enslaved people of Mount Vernon.

Careful reading of Washington's papers reveals the extent to which his and his family's lives were intimately intertwined with those of the enslaved people who surrounded them and labored for them—operating the plantation's economic enterprises, supporting the household's legendary hospitality, and, to a large degree, underpinning Washington's influential public service. The well-documented role of slavery in Washington's life makes all the more remarkable the bold gesture that he made near the end of his life, when he wrote into his 1799 will a clause that provided for freedom to be granted to the slaves that he owned. Of the eight presidents of the United States who owned slaves while in office, he was the only one to take such action. Recognizing that his actions were the subject of public scrutiny, he certainly intended this particular action to be precedent-setting, signaling his opposition to slavery and his hope for its eventual abolition.

Ann Pamela Cunningham also set an important precedent by insisting on preserving Mount Vernon's outbuildings, despite "expert" advice that only the Mansion and the Washingtons' tomb were worthy of saving. Today these rare work structures provide invaluable physical evidence and context of everyday life on the plantation. The placement of a memorial stone at the site of Mount Vernon's slave cemetery in 1929 stands out as an early effort by a historical site to acknowledge and pay tribute to the enslaved. In 1962, the opening of a living quarter in one wing of the reconstructed brick greenhouse represented a similarly early attempt to offer insights into their daily experiences. Two decades later, the Mount Vernon Ladies' Association erected at the cemetery a more extensive memorial, designed by Howard University architecture students. Creation of a professional archaeology department soon followed, with the primary mission of investigating physical and documentary evidence on slavery. In 1994, Mount Vernon hosted a scholarly conference on "Slavery in the Life of Washington," later published as *Slavery at the Home of George Washington*. The following year saw the introduction of a "slave life tour," often led by Gladys Quander Tancil, Mount Vernon's first African American historical interpreter. Ongoing research has informed both the opening of a reconstructed slave cabin, suggesting the living conditions of field workers, and the refurbishment of the greenhouse slave quarter. Most recently, new technologies have facilitated the creation of a database to collect period documentation of slavery and the initiation of a non-invasive archaeological survey to determine the number and arrangement of graves in the slave cemetery, so that these can be better recognized and commemorated.

Building upon this long tradition of research and interpretation, *Lives Bound Together* marks the first major exhibition focused on slavery at Mount Vernon and George Washington's evolving views on slavery in general. Drawing on the capacity of digital technology to connect thousands of primary source references, the exhibition features biographical sketches, in unprecedented detail, of nineteen enslaved individuals.

As one of the best preserved and most thoroughly documented of all eighteenth-century American plantations, Mount Vernon continues, through *Lives Bound Together*, to play a vital part in continuing discussions of America's history, meaning, and future.

Barbara B. Lucas
Regent, The Mount Vernon Ladies' Association
Vice Regent for Maryland

Acknowledgments

This publication, and the exhibition that inspires it, represent significant undertakings, realized only through the collaborative efforts of a large cast of Mount Vernon staff, volunteers, board members, scholars, advisors, descendants, and supporters. At the head of the list is Mount Vernon's Research Historian, Mary V. Thompson, who has devoted decades to studying virtually every aspect of slavery at Mount Vernon—from George Washington's changing views, to the day-to-day experiences of those enslaved on the estate, to locating and making connections with descendants of the enslaved. We cannot thank her enough for her unfailing generosity in sharing her research.

Associate Curator Jessie MacLeod has acted as both lead curator for the exhibition and the primary author of this publication, writing biographical profiles that afford us glimpses into the lives of eighteen enslaved men and women and one child. Combining energy, passion, superb writing skills, and training in public history, Jessie has accomplished the presentation of a complex and difficult historical subject in an accessible and sensitive manner. Administrator Hannah Freece has been an essential collaborator in matters of both ideas and implementation; it is hard to imagine how we could have functioned without her initiative, her efficient coordination of details, or her reminders of deadlines.

Book designer Wynne Patterson skillfully combined words and images to produce a visually appealing and inviting volume; Sally Wern Comport created the silhouettes that grace the biographical profiles. Dawn Bonner assembled images and secured permissions, with her usual aplomb and good cheer; Mary Ellen Wilson copyedited the text; Robie Grant compiled the index.

The development of *Lives Bound Together: Slavery at George Washington's Mount Vernon* has benefitted significantly from the insights of an Advisory Committee that includes Dr. William B. Allen, Dr. Nancy Bercaw, Mrs. Alpha Coles Blackburn, Kristin Gallas, Dr. Paul Gardullo, and Dr. Dianne Swann-Wright. Three of the advisors—Dr. Scott E. Casper, Dr. Maurie D. McInnis, and Judge Rohulamin Quander—also wrote essays for this publication, adding their perspectives to those offered by Dr.

Eleanor Breen, Gloria Tancil Holmes, Molly H. Kerr, ZSun-nee Matema, Dr. Philip D. Morgan, and Dr. Esther C. White. We are further grateful to Dr. Annette Gordon-Reed, Harvard University, for her thoughtful introduction.

Two ongoing research initiatives have contributed significantly to the ideas and information presented in *Lives Bound Together*: the creation of a digital humanities database designed to bring together all primary source references to the lives and work of the enslaved people of Mount Vernon; and a systematic survey of the plantation's slave cemetery, aimed at mapping, marking, and commemorating the final resting places of Mount Vernon's enslaved residents. Both of these initiatives originated in Mount Vernon's archaeology program, led today by Dr. Luke Pecararo. Molly Kerr joined the staff in 2013 to oversee design and implementation of the Mount Vernon slavery database; she recruited and led a team of volunteers who contributed thousands of hours to logging primary source information: Virginia Adams, Betsy Alexander, Catherine Amos, Lori Arbuckle, Sara Collini, Bethany Critchley, Patricia Duffy, Adam Dzierwa, Kevin Gushman, Joi Kudirka, Alexandra Levy, Kara Lobley, Christopher Martin, Kristin Mattice, Raymond Niederhausen, Penelope Norton, Meghan Olson, Nicky Resch, Rebecca Schumann, Kerrie Simpson, Richard Smith, Kara Wheeler, Parker White, and Stephanie Will; Barry Burr designed the database. Other volunteers—too numerous to list—joined staff archaeologists in the search for traces of burials in the slave cemetery.

Shortly after we began planning the exhibition, we realized that the importance of the topic and the extent of supporting materials merited a larger space than the single gallery previously allocated to special exhibitions. *Lives Bound Together* thus encompasses all seven galleries in the museum wing of the Donald W. Reynolds Museum and Education Center, making this the most ambitious special exhibition that Mount Vernon has mounted since the 2006 opening of that facility.

The vast majority of exhibition items come from Mount Vernon's existing holdings of fine and decorative arts, archaeological materials, and library special collections. We are grateful to the many donors and lenders who over the years have made it possible for so many original Washington materials to return to the estate. We are particularly indebted to the Museo Thyssen-Bornemisza, Madrid, for granting the important international loan of the *Portrait of George Washington's Cook*, for the opening six months of *Lives Bound Together*. Original documents and other items from the Fairfax County Circuit Court; Gilder Lehrman Collection; the Library of Congress; Morristown National Historical Park; the National Archives and Records Administration; National Museum of American History, Smithsonian Institution; New Hampshire Historical Society; Yale University Art Gallery, de Lancey Kountze Collection; and David

M. Rubenstein, provide an unparalleled window onto the subject. For their assistance in arranging institutional loans, we thank Barbara Bair, Guillermo Solano, Marian Aparicio, Lucia Cassol, Thaddeus I. Gray, Marco Grassi, Seth Kaller, Katrina Krempasky, Sandra Trenholm, Jude Pfister, Rachel Waldron, and James Zeender. We are also indebted to Loretta Carter Hanes and Peter Hanes for the loan of two china bowls treasured by generations of their family.

Exhibitions Registrar Diana Welsh competently and with impressive calm managed the myriad tasks relating to exhibition loans, fabrication, and installation, with the assistance of the Collections Management team, led by Elizabeth Chambers. Collections Conservator Karl Knauer adroitly oversaw all object conservation concerns and treatments, assisted by Sophie Hunter. Karen Price photographed archaeological objects. Savannah McMullen developed content for the interactive components of the exhibition, synthesizing extensive research into readable, engaging biographies while providing context and prompting visitors to think about the complex choices faced by both George Washington and enslaved people at Mount Vernon. Dr. Douglas Bradburn, Founding Director of the Fred W. Smith National Library for the Study of George Washington, offered insightful comments on the exhibition script. Linda Baumgarten, Dr. John J. McCusker, and Bruce Ragsdale generously shared their expertise on costume, price calculations, and agriculture.

Charles Mack, exhibition designer, and Sally Wern Comport, graphics designer, sensitively translated our abstract ideas into engaging three-dimensional experiences; we are grateful for their counsel, their creativity, and their flexibility. We thank Bruce Lee, Dermot Rooney, and their colleagues at ELY, Inc., for their skilled mountmaking and art handling; and Scott Jackson, Betty Jo Kaveney, Mike Page, and associates at Blair, Inc. for exhibit fabrication and graphic production. Joe Sliger, John Davis, and Mount Vernon's Operations and Maintenance crew provided vital assistance with case construction, exhibit fabrication, electrical work, and painting. Samantha McCarty and Neal Hurst constructed reproduction clothing; Hoag and Sandy Levins created faux foods. For touch screen interactives, oral history videos, exhibition website, and other digital components that enliven the exhibition experience and vastly expand its impact, we thank Robert Shenk, Matt Briney, Lisa Cassell, Will Cotton, and Mason Shelby. Alex Herder and Ric Cunningham of the Duke and the Duck spearheaded production of the introductory video.

Marion Dobbins conducted oral history interviews with descendants of men and women enslaved at Mount Vernon, including Ann Chinn, Shawn Costley, Phyllis Walker Ford, Stephen Hammond, ZSun-nee Matema, Jay Quander, and Judge Rohulamin Quander. We are much indebted to these individuals for their willingness to share individual reflections and family stories, which provide personal connections that no archival documents can match. Conversations both formal and informal taught us much, and we are especially grateful to Sheila Bryant Coates, Audrey P. Davis, Larry Earl, Dr. Gwen Everett, Brenda Faison, Carolyn Felder-Hines, Kelley Green, Ed Hines, Guin Jones, Richard Josey, Daniel Lee, Christopher Reynolds, and the participants in Mount Vernon teacher institutes and outreach sessions at the Alexandria Black History Museum.

For their essential support and encouragement of *Lives Bound Together* and related initiatives, we thank Curtis G. Viebranz, President of George Washington's Mount Vernon, and Carol Borchert Cadou, Senior Vice President for Historic Preservation and Collections. Numerous colleagues from across the estate contributed to these projects in various ways: Eric Benson, Joe Downer, Jillian Barto, Tyler Branscome, Mark Santangelo, Rebecca Baird, Michele Lee, Allison Wickens, Jamie Bosket, Linda Powell, Steven T. Bashore, Kathrin Breitt Brown, Sam Murphy, Rebecca Aloisi, Melissa Wood, Elizabeth Salamon, Susan Magill, F. Anderson Morse, and Kristen Otto.

We are especially pleased to recognize and thank the Nimick Forbesway Foundation for generously funding this publication. For support of the exhibition, we thank Ambassador and Mrs. Nicholas F. Taubman, Dr. Scholl Foundation, Nimick Forbesway Foundation, an anonymous donor, Maribeth and Wm. Harold Borthwick, the Challenge Foundation, Mr. Paul Neely, Catherine M. and Frederick H. Waddell, and the Honorable and Mrs. Togo D. West, Jr. We also thank George Overend and others who worked behind-the-scenes to facilitate the funding of this project. The Life Guard Society of Mount Vernon, under the leadership of Jo Carol Porter, provided initial funding for the digital humanities database.

Finally, none of this would have been possible without the backing of the Mount Vernon Ladies' Association, which has owned and operated George Washington's Mount Vernon since 1860, with the entwined goals of preservation and education. We are grateful for the leadership of Barbara Lucas, Regent 2013–2016, and Vice Regent for Maryland; her predecessor, Ann Bookout, Regent 2010–2013, and Vice Regent for Texas; and the chairs of the Collections Committee, Andrea Sahin, Vice Regent for Massachusetts, and Susan Townsend, Vice Regent for Delaware—and for the support and encouragement of Vice Regents from throughout the nation.

Susan P. Schoelwer
Robert H. Smith Senior Curator
George Washington's Mount Vernon

Introduction

Annette Gordon-Reed

Mount Vernon is well known as the home of George Washington, the commander of the Continental Army, who led the American colonies to victory in the Revolutionary War, who served as president of the Constitutional Convention, and then went on to become the first president of the United States. Over the years, millions of visitors have come to his home on the Potomac, hoping to discover something about the man that may have (or almost surely) escaped capture in the voluminous body of writing about him.

Lives Bound Together: Slavery at George Washington's Mount Vernon reminds us that the man who was "first in war, first in peace, and first in the hearts of his countrymen" had another important title and role. He was the legal owner, over the course of his life, of hundreds of enslaved black people—men, women, and children. As this volume reminds us, the institution of "slavery was an integral part of George Washington's world." As a result, it is impossible to tell a truthful story—one that is as complete as it can be—about a world in which chattel slavery flourished without telling the story of the people Washington enslaved at his home and in other places where he lived and spent time.

Much has been written about Washington as a slaveholder—what he thought, how his views did or did not change over time. Unlike his fellow Virginian Thomas Jefferson, whose nearly five decades' worth of entanglements with the Hemings family has riveted interest on individuals enslaved at Monticello since the 1970s, much less attention has been paid to those enslaved at Mount Vernon. The brief biographies presented in these pages seek to reveal their stories for considered view, providing a different perspective on enslavement at George Washington's plantation. Here we see slavery through the eyes of nineteen individuals who were the objects of the institution's depredations. We are moved to imagine and understand, as much as is humanly possible, what their lives were like. Each person had unique experiences, from spending time engaged in domestic work in the Mansion, to acting as personal servants to George and Martha Washington, to working in the fields or as artisans, doing whatever tasks the Washingtons compelled them to perform. The bottom line of their lives, however, was the same: they were, by law, unable to leave the couple's service, unable to guard against the breaking up of their families, and they could be, and often were, physically punished—sometimes even sold to the Caribbean—if they disobeyed orders, made mistakes, or otherwise caused conflict.

We see the effects of ancient property rules on the families of the enslaved. Martha, the widow of Daniel Parke Custis when she married George Washington, came to the marriage with dower interests in enslaved people. Living and laboring together, a number of these so-called "dower slaves" married and had children with people legally owned by George Washington. These relationships eventually caused great complications and heartbreak, for when Martha died, the Custis heirs inherited the dower slaves, some of whom, like Frank and Lucy Lee and their children Mike, Philip, and Patty, were parceled out to different households, with Philip being sent the farthest away. Frank Lee, whom Washington had legally owned, was freed by the terms of Washington's will. Determined to stay as close to his family as he could, Lee was forced to choose between being near Lucy, Mike, and Patty or near Philip. He decided to live near the former.

The personal histories presented in *Lives Bound Together* explode any notion that physical proximity to the slaveholder, and any so-called privileges enslaved people were given, dampened the desire for liberty or stood as certain protection against capricious cruelty. Hercules, the Washingtons' famous chef who cooked for the couple at Mount Vernon and in Philadelphia, was given "the perk[s] of his position," selling "'leftovers' from the kitchen . . . which were often used for industrial purposes in the eighteenth century." He was known for the fine clothing he bought with the money he received. Yet that all ended abruptly when Washington, who had been shuttling enslaved people in and out of Philadelphia to avoid the effects of the residency rule written into the state's gradual emancipation statute, sent the proud chef back to Mount Vernon and "assigned [him] to digging ditches, crushing gravel, making bricks, and weeding the garden." Hercules eventually escaped, and though Washington tried to recapture him, he was never found. The story of Ona Judge Staines, lady's maid to Martha Washington, who also successfully escaped and was the subject of the Washingtons' most persistent effort at recovery, provides an excellent view into the mindset of an enslaved person and that of the Washingtons as well.

One is struck by the number of people described in this book who attempted freedom, and the number of times they tried, though in a few cases they were "not running away—they were running to," seeking to be with relatives and friends near Mount Vernon. What comes through clearly is the desperation to form and maintain family and community ties. Field-workers could be assigned to any one of Mount Vernon's five farms without regard to the assignments of their wives, husbands, or children. Efforts had to be made, and often were, to share whatever free time they could get to be with loved ones.

The extremely insightful essays that appear after the biographies of the enslaved raise vital questions. They also provide context and present additional information about the nature of slavery at Mount Vernon. They further make clear, in ways that it was not to some in the past, that slavery was the reason this plantation existed and what made its existence possible over the decades. The enslaved people who lived there—what they did, how their lives unfolded, how they attempted to order their lives, and what actions the Washingtons took to control their lives—must be an integral part of any story that is told about this place. The material and analyses presented herein remind us that we do not yet have, but do sorely need, what could be a called a *definitive* monograph on slavery, George Washington, and Mount Vernon. This excellent volume is foundational, and it will almost certainly be the spark to create such a much-needed work.

Lives Bound Together

Introduction to Part One

The rich textual and material evidence that has long supported research and writing about the lives of George and Martha Washington also includes a wealth of information about the enslaved men, women, and children of their Mount Vernon plantation. Because of proximity to the most famous American of his time, the lives of the enslaved people of Mount Vernon can be glimpsed in greater detail than any comparable group of slaves in eighteenth-century America. Indeed, it can be said that George Washington wrote the biographies of Mount Vernon's enslaved people.

Thousands of references in his voluminous papers make it possible to trace the experiences of specific individuals through time and follow family lineages through multiple generations. Visitor descriptions, public records, oral histories, and archaeology fill in some of the blanks. The resulting level of personal history is unparalleled, contrasting with the isolated references and faceless statistics that are all we have to illuminate the lives of the vast majority of eighteenth-century enslaved Americans.

In the pages that follow, Mount Vernon curator Jessie MacLeod introduces nineteen individuals from Mount Vernon's enslaved community. Some are far better documented than others. Those who worked as personal attendants, household servants, and artisans tend to be the best represented in surviving documents, because they interacted more closely with the Washingtons and were more often observed by visitors. Despite such disparities, the selection of biographical subjects tries to suggest a range of experiences. Thus, we meet both men and women; natives of Africa and the Virginia Tidewater; field-workers, craftsmen, and domestic laborers; some who traveled as far as Boston or Charleston, and some who never left the immediate vicinity of Mount Vernon; some who succeeded in escaping and some who were recaptured and sold as punishment; some who died in slavery and some who became free. Presented in clusters that correspond to galleries in the exhibition that inspired this publication, these biographies underline the degree to which the Washingtons' personal lives and George Washington's public career, were, like the larger history of America, inextricably entwined with, and supported by, enslaved labor.

Enslaved People of Mount Vernon:
Biographies

Jessie MacLeod

Slavery and George Washington's World

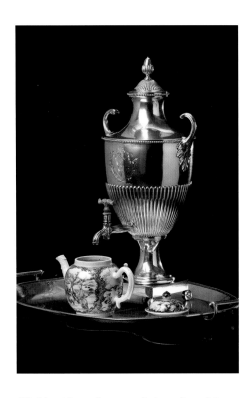

World-wide trade networks brought to Mount Vernon silver from London, porcelain from China, tea from Asia, sugar from the West Indies, and labor from Africa.

OVERLEAF: *Edward Savage's painting of the* West Front of Mount Vernon, *ca. 1787–92, features the Washington family enjoying the Mansion grounds. Behind them, an enslaved woman (center) and a group of enslaved men (left) go about their daily work.*

Slavery was an integral part of George Washington's world. Like his elite contemporaries, Washington participated in a global commercial system in which the slave trade and enslaved labor played a key part. At Mount Vernon, enslaved workers in the Mansion, craft workshops, and fields performed essential labor that supported the Washingtons' lifestyle and created much of their wealth. Even as George Washington began to feel ambivalent about slavery during the Revolutionary War, the institution retained a deep hold on his daily life.

Transatlantic trade in the eighteenth century involved the flow of raw materials from the Americas, finished goods from Europe, and captured people from Africa. George Washington was enmeshed in this system as both a consumer and a producer. In the decades before the Revolutionary War, he purchased captive Africans and their descendants to work in his household and farm his land. Throughout his life, Washington bought imported products like sugar, rum, coffee, and chocolate—which were harvested by enslaved Africans in the Caribbean—along with the silver, glass, and porcelain accoutrements to serve these items in his home. In later years, Washington sent barrels of salted fish (caught in the Potomac by his enslaved workforce) to the Caribbean, where plantation owners purchased them to feed their slaves. On several occasions, Washington punished his enslaved workers by sending them to be sold in the West Indies.

Slavery was also a fundamental part of Mount Vernon's operations. In 1799, 317 men, women, and children lived in bondage on Mount Vernon's five farms, vastly outnumbering the twenty or so Washington family members and hired white laborers. Enslaved domestic workers were "on call" at all times and a constant presence in the Mansion. Valets and chambermaids such as William Lee and Oney Judge assisted George and Martha Washington with such intimate tasks as dressing and bathing, while nannies like Molly cared for the Custis children and grandchildren. Frank Lee, Caroline Branham, Doll, and others cleaned the Washingtons' home, cooked their meals, and served the family and guests in Mount Vernon's dining room, parlors, and bedrooms.[1] As they scrubbed, dusted, and polished, these enslaved people interacted with many of the family's elegant furnishings and tablewares as much as, if not more than, the Washingtons themselves.

The vast majority of enslaved workers labored outside the Mansion. Sambo Anderson, Priscilla, Kate, Davy Gray, Caesar, and hundreds of other craftspeople and field-workers constructed and repaired the estate's buildings, planted and harvested crops, produced tools and clothing, cared for livestock, and maintained the landscape. The profits from their labor made possible the Washingtons' elite lifestyle, expressed in the costly furnishings that filled Mount Vernon's rooms. The work of enslaved people also allowed George Washington to leave his estate for months at a time to serve the country as general and president. As human property, their bodies formed a significant portion of his wealth.

John Evans's New Map of the World, *1799.*

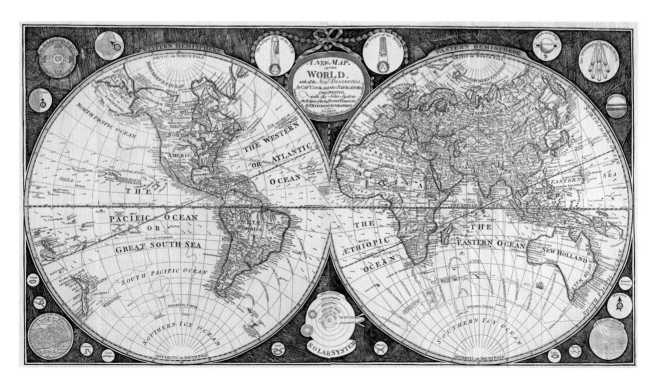

Frank Lee

This small room next to Mount Vernon's dining room was described in 1799 as "the closet under Franks direction."

Frank Lee came to Mount Vernon in 1768 after George Washington purchased him from Mary Lee, a widow who lived eighty miles away in Westmoreland County, Virginia. Washington paid £50 for the young man, about the cost of three good horses. He also bought Frank's older brother William Lee, who would become Washington's longtime personal valet.[2]

Both Frank and William Lee were described as "mulatto," meaning that they were mixed race, likely the children of an enslaved woman and a white man.[3] It was common at Mount Vernon and other southern plantations for light-skinned slaves to receive work assignments in the house. More than 6 percent of Mount Vernon's enslaved population were described as "mulatto," about average for Virginia in this period.[4]

Frank Lee was assigned first to be a waiter in the Mansion and, later, to the relatively high-prestige position of butler. As butler, Lee played an essential role in the household. He oversaw the Washingtons' tableware, waited on the family at meals, monitored the stores of food and wine, supervised the cleaning of the house, and looked after some of the estate's dogs. Lee was usually the first person a visitor to Mount Vernon saw. Wearing the white-and-red livery suit of the Washington household, he greeted guests and announced their presence to the family. One visitor commented on his "politeness and kindness."[5] The 1799 inventory of Mount Vernon describes the closet off the dining room as "the closet under Franks direction," an indication of his authority over this part of Mount Vernon's operations.[6]

Frank Lee no doubt knew that his position inside the house required him to be both omnipresent and invisible. When the architect Benjamin Henry Latrobe visited the estate in July 1796, he enjoyed coffee with the Washington family one evening on the piazza. In a sketch of the event, Latrobe included an enslaved man, quite possibly Lee, behind the fully set table. In Latrobe's final watercolor of the scene, this figure is missing.[7]

After arriving at Mount Vernon, Lee married into one of the largest multigenerational families on the estate. His wife, Lucy, was the daughter of Doll, Mount Vernon's longtime cook. Lucy's sister Alce (likely pronounced "Al-sie"), was the mother of Christopher Sheels, who became Washington's valet when William Lee sustained crippling injuries.

In 1799 Frank and Lucy had three children: Mike, Philip, and Patty. A fourth child, Edmund, is mentioned in earlier records but may have died in the 1790s. For a time, Frank and Lucy's family lived in a room above the kitchen.[8] By 1799 this room was occupied by the hired white housekeeper, Mrs. Forbes, so the Lee family may have moved to one of the small wooden cabins near the Mansion. Documents also refer to Frank having a "room" in the cellar of the Mansion.[9] This may have been an office space or possibly where he slept when he was needed in the house.

Because ownership was passed through the maternal line, Lucy and her children belonged to the Custis estate. Frank Lee was owned by George Washington, so he received his freedom in 1801 by the terms of Washington's will. Lucy and their children remained enslaved. In 1802, after Martha Washington's death, Lucy, Mike, and Patty were inherited by Martha's granddaughter Eleanor (Nelly) Parke Custis Lewis, who lived at nearby Woodlawn plantation. Philip Lee, then seventeen years old, was separated from his family and sent to Arlington House, where he became valet to Martha's grandson George Washington Parke Custis.[10]

For the next nineteen years, Frank stayed in the vicinity of Mount Vernon, presumably to be close to his wife and two children at Woodlawn. When he died in 1821, this announcement appeared in the *Alexandria Gazette*: "DIED. Lately at Mount Vernon, at a very advanced age, Francis Lee, Butler to that mansion in the days of its ancient master."[11]

Two views of the Washington family on the piazza in July 1796, drawn by British architect Benjamin Henry Latrobe (details). The initial sketch (left) includes an enslaved man, standing behind the table, a figure omitted from the final watercolor (right).

Frank Lee's obituary, 1821.

DIED.
Lately at Mount Vernon, at a very advanced age, Francis Lee, Butler to that mansion in the days of its ancient master. Francis was the brother of William Lee, body servant to the General, in the war of the Revolution, and particularly mentioned in the general's will.

Doll

In 1759, Doll traveled about 120 miles, following her mistress to a new home at Mount Vernon.

Doll was thirty-eight years old when she arrived at Mount Vernon in 1759. She and her children were among the more than 80 enslaved people whom Martha Dandridge Custis brought to her marriage to George Washington, as part of her "dower" or widow's share of her first husband's estate. Many of the "dower" slaves remained on Custis properties, but about 20 household workers and craftsmen were taken to Mount Vernon from their previous home in New Kent County, Virginia.[12] Doll and her fellow Custis slaves had to adjust to a new life—and a new community—on Washington's plantation.

As the estate's cook for many years, Doll worked long hours in the kitchen preparing the hoecakes, smoked hams, and other Washington family favorites. It is likely that Martha Washington installed Doll as cook because she was familiar with the enslaved woman's skills. Mount Vernon's steady stream of visitors meant that Doll frequently had to prepare large and elaborate meals. She worked closely with Martha to plan each day's menu and monitor ingredients. Though under her mistress's supervision, the kitchen was Doll's domain. She passed on her expertise to her daughter Lucy, who succeeded her mother as one of the estate's cooks.

By the 1780s, Doll no longer had a formal work assignment.[13] Then in her sixties, she likely assisted with knitting and mending, tasks that Washington often assigned to elderly slaves. She continued to use the kitchen to distill rose and mint water for medicinal purposes and to dry fruits such as cherries.[14] She also sold chickens and ducks to George Washington, as did many enslaved people on the estate.

Doll was the matriarch of one of the largest extended families within Mount Vernon's enslaved community. In 1799 she had six children—Will, George, Doll, Lucy, Peter, and Alce—as well as seventeen grandchildren and at least six great-grandchildren living on the estate. Her daughter Lucy married Frank Lee, the enslaved butler. Her grandson Christopher Sheels became Washington's personal valet.

Because she was owned by the Custis estate, Doll remained enslaved after Martha Washington's death. She may have been inherited by Elizabeth (Eliza) Parke Custis Law or George Washington Parke Custis.[15] On the list of the division of the Custis slaves, both inherited a "Doll" or "Dolly" valued at just £5, a low figure indicating that the women were elderly.[16] By 1802 Doll would have been eighty-one years old.

4:00AM   *Doll, the Washingtons' cook, wakes up in her quarters.*

4:30AM   *She revives the fire in the kitchen, and draws and heats water.*

6:00AM   *Doll prepares hoecakes (cornmeal pancakes), coffee, tea, and drinking chocolate for breakfast. She demonstrates her methods to Hercules, a young enslaved man she is training to be a cook.*

6:30AM   *Martha Washington visits the kitchen to ensure that breakfast is underway. Enslaved waiter Frank Lee sets the table for breakfast.*

7:00AM   *The bell rings to announce that breakfast is served in the dining room. The Washington family and their guests sit down to eat.*

7:30AM   *Schomberg, an enslaved laborer at Mansion House Farm, stops by the kitchen to drop off ripe fruits and vegetables from the garden.*

8:00AM   *Frank Lee clears the table in the dining room. Doll and her assistant, her teenaged daughter Lucy, clean pots and pans. Martha Washington returns to the kitchen to discuss the dinner menu with Doll. They select a turkey for dinner.*

9:00AM   *Doll begins preparing the turkey and instructs Hercules to wash and chop the vegetables.*

12:00PM   *Doll takes a few minutes to sit down between tasks. Picking up her knitting, she resumes work on a pair of stockings.*

2:00PM   *Doll bakes bread while Hercules tends the iron and copper pots in the fireplace. Martha Washington visits the kitchen to oversee dinner preparations.*

2:45PM   *The plantation bell rings to alert the Washingtons and their guests that dinner is ready. Doll and Hercules transfer foods into serving dishes and platters. Waiters Frank Lee and Breechy carry the dishes to the dining room.*

3:00PM   *The Washingtons and their guests enjoy dinner. Doll, Hercules, and Lucy eat dinner in the kitchen.*

4:30PM   *Frank Lee and the waiters clear the table and clean the dining room. Doll organizes the kitchen as her daughter Lucy washes dishes.*

5:00PM   *Hercules chops wood for use in the kitchen the next day.*

6:00PM   *Doll and Hercules brew tea and slice bread and leftover cold meat for tea.*

6:30PM   *Frank Lee and Breechy serve tea to the Washingtons.*

7:00PM   *Martha Washington oversees as Doll measures ingredients and mixes bread dough and hoecake batter for the next day.*

8:00PM   *Doll cleans the kitchen and banks the fire for the night. She returns to her quarters to see the rest of her children, tend to her personal garden, and rest.*

Interior of the Mount Vernon kitchen today.

Conjectural timeline based on 18th-century documentation.

Caroline Branham

Emptying chamber pots was just one of an enslaved housemaid's many duties.

In June 1796, George Washington sent instructions to his farm manager William Pearce for preparing the Mount Vernon Mansion for the family's arrival from Philadelphia. He told Pearce to have the rooms in the servants' hall cleaned and the beds put in order, to attach a lock on the door, and to "order Caroline, or whoever has the charge of those rooms, to suffer no person to sleep, or even to go into it, without express orders from her Mistress or myself."[17]

Washington's reference to the enslaved housemaid Caroline Branham illuminates the role she played in cleaning, maintaining, and protecting the rooms of the Mansion and its associated structures. Caroline, Molly, Charlotte, and other enslaved housemaids faced a relentless cycle of domestic work: lighting fires, making beds, washing clothes and linens, sweeping and scrubbing floors, and dusting furniture, among many other duties. George Washington expected them to be productive even when not performing household work. Branham was also a seamstress, sewing household linens and such clothing as shirts and shifts for her fellow enslaved workers.

The recollections of Hannah Taylor, a resident of Alexandria, provide an intimate glimpse of Branham's role in the house. As a seven-year-old girl, Taylor accidentally fell asleep in Washington's carriage when it was in Alexandria for repairs. She did not awaken until the carriage arrived at Mount Vernon, at which point it was late and stormy, prompting the Washingtons to insist that she stay the night (they sent an enslaved messenger to alert her parents). After dining with the family, Taylor told an interviewer years later, "Caroline Brannum, a colored maid … took her to a little room at the head of the stairway. She then brought a copper warming-pan, the first Hannah had ever seen, and ran it between the sheets of the bed, and produced a nightgown of Miss Nelly's and put it on the little girl…. She was covered up and tucked in the feather bed, and Caroline left the candle burning until Hannah had gone to sleep." The next morning, "Mrs. Washington told Caroline to have a brick heated and put in the coach, which was waiting at the door to take Hannah home to Alexandria."[18]

Given the large number of visitors each year, Branham had many guests—not to mention the Washington family—for whom to fetch warming pans, light fires and candles, provide fresh jugs of water for

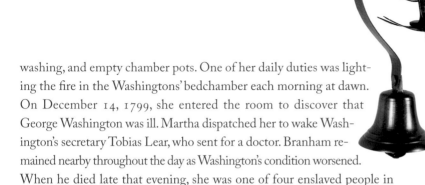

washing, and empty chamber pots. One of her daily duties was lighting the fire in the Washingtons' bedchamber each morning at dawn. On December 14, 1799, she entered the room to discover that George Washington was ill. Martha dispatched her to wake Washington's secretary Tobias Lear, who sent for a doctor. Branham remained nearby throughout the day as Washington's condition worsened. When he died late that evening, she was one of four enslaved people in the room.[19]

Originally hung on the south end of the Mansion, this bell rang to alert house slaves that they were needed for some task.

Caroline Branham was married to Peter Hardiman, an enslaved groom whom Washington rented for £12 per year from David Stuart, who had married the widow of Martha's son, John (Jacky) Parke Custis.[20] Though there was no guarantee they could stay together, Caroline and Peter benefited from Washington's preference to keep enslaved families intact. In 1788 Washington wrote to Stuart that he was hiring Peter that year "as well on acc[oun]t of my Jacks, Stud Horses, Mares, etc., as because he seems unwilling to part with his wife and Children."[21] By that time the couple had two children, two-year-old Wilson and one-year-old Rachel. They later had at least six more: Jemima, Leanthe, Polly, Peter, Austin, and Daniel.

After Martha Washington's death in 1802, Caroline Branham and her children were inherited by George Washington Parke Custis. Peter Hardiman was also inherited by Custis, allowing the family to stay together.[22]

The "little room at the head of the stairs," where Caroline Branham tucked in Hannah Taylor.

Soldier, Statesman, Slaveholder

Edward Savage's group portrait of The Washington
Family, *engraved in 1798, with an unidentified enslaved
man wearing a livery suit.*

George Washington's views on slavery changed gradually and dramatically over the course of his life.[23] As a young Virginia planter, he accepted slavery without apparent hesitation. During the Revolutionary War, he began to express doubts about the institution. Throughout the 1780s and 1790s, Washington stated in private correspondence that he no longer wanted to be a slave owner, that he did not want to buy and sell slaves or separate enslaved families, and that he supported a plan for gradual abolition in the United States. He also began exploring ways to emancipate his slaves—a task complicated by the presence at Mount Vernon of many enslaved people belonging to the Custis estate, whom Washington was legally unable to free.

Yet Washington's relationship to slavery was complex, and his actions did not always correspond to his growing antislavery principles. At the Constitutional Convention and later as president, he tried to remain neutral in the heated national debates over the issue, and he did not publicly advocate for abolition. His first priorities were maintaining the young nation's fragile union and upholding the property rights of slaveholders. In 1793 he signed into law the federal Fugitive Slave Act, which allowed owners to pursue runaway slaves across state lines. The following year, he signed legislation limiting American involvement in the transatlantic slave trade.[24] On a personal level, he strategically rotated the executive household's enslaved workers out of Pennsylvania to evade that state's 1780 emancipation law, which declared that slaves residing in the state for more than six months could claim their freedom (all but two were owned by the Custis estate, so Washington would have been liable for their value if they escaped).

For those enslaved at Mount Vernon and at the president's house in Philadelphia, their master's internal conflict did not alter their bondage. As Washington's public profile rose, enslaved people like his valet William Lee and cook Hercules became prominent figures in their own right and responded to their enslavement in very different ways.

William (Billy) Lee

Portrait of George Washington *by John Trumbull, 1780. The man in the background may represent William Lee, although the turban is an artistic flourish.*

William (Billy) Lee came to Mount Vernon in 1768, after Washington purchased him from Mary Lee, a Virginia widow, for £61.15s. Washington also bought William's younger brother Frank, who went on to serve as a waiter and butler in the household. Both William and Frank were described as "mulatto," or mixed race, meaning they were probably the sons of an enslaved mother and a white father.[25]

For two decades, William Lee accompanied Washington nearly everywhere. As manservant, or valet, Lee assisted his master with myriad tasks, from delivering messages to laying out clothes to tying a silk ribbon around his hair. An excellent horseman who was described as muscular and athletic, Lee also rode in Washington's beloved fox hunts.[26]

William Lee served with Washington throughout the Revolutionary War. He was responsible for organizing the general's personal affairs, including his voluminous papers, and holding his spyglass. As the attendant to a prominent figure, Lee became a minor celebrity. Postwar visitors to Mount Vernon occasionally sought out the "famed body-servant of the commander-in-chief."[27]

Spending more than eight years in close proximity during the intensity of war seems to have made Washington and Lee's relationship especially close. The former's views on slavery shifted significantly during the war, and he emerged with a newfound abhorrence of slavery and a commitment to neither buy nor sell slaves and to avoid separating enslaved families. Many factors likely influenced Washington's evolution, but his close relationship with William Lee may have helped him understand more fully the humanity of those he enslaved.

During the Revolution, Lee married a free black woman named Margaret Thomas from Philadelphia. Thomas had worked for Washington's household as a seamstress and washerwoman. After the war, Lee asked his owner to bring Thomas to Mount Vernon. Although Washington grumbled that he "never wished to see her more," he acquiesced, noting that he could not refuse his valet's request "(if it can be complied with on reasonable terms) as he has lived with me so long and followed my fortunes with fidelity." There is no evidence, however, that Margaret Thomas ever lived at Mount Vernon. Washington's correspondence notes that she had been in "ill health," so she may have passed away before or shortly after arrival.[28]

In the mid-1780s, William Lee endured several accidents that severely damaged both of his knees.[29] Despite his disability, he insisted on traveling to New York to join Washington in the executive household. When his condition worsened on the journey, he was forced to stop in Philadelphia, where doctors fitted him with a steel brace. Washington's affection for Lee is clear in correspondence between his secretary and agent in Philadelphia as they conferred on Lee's situation. Washington's secretary wrote, "if he is still anxious to come on here the President would gratify

William Lee's duties as Washington's valet included laying out toiletries, preparing clothing, and dressing his master's hair.

William Lee accompanied General Washington on his travels throughout the Revolutionary War.

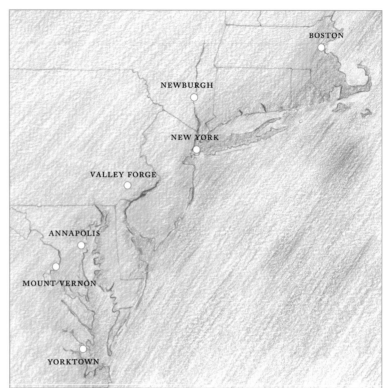

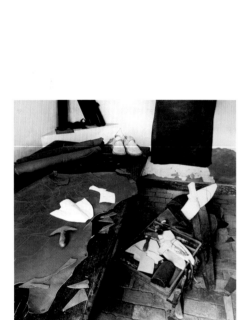

The shoemaker's shop in Mount Vernon's greenhouse slave quarter, where William Lee was assigned to work after injuring his knees.

him altho' he will be troublesome. He has been an old & faithful Servt. This is enough for the Presidt to gratify him in every reasonable wish."[30]

Though a determined Lee finally reached New York two months later, it soon became clear that he was no longer physically able to act as Washington's valet. He was sent back to Mount Vernon and became the estate's shoemaker, working in the small cobbler shop behind the greenhouse.[31] It is unclear, and perhaps impossible to know, whether Lee's devotion to Washington stemmed from genuine affection or the desire to maintain a position of relative privilege within the enslaved community.

Washington certainly believed the former. When the retired president died, William Lee was the only slave freed immediately in his will. Washington provided Lee with an annual allowance of $30 for the rest of his life, noting, "this I give him as a testimony of my sense of his attachment to me, and for his faithful services during the Revolutionary War."[32] Lee remained on the estate until his own death in 1810.[33] He is believed to be buried in the slave cemetery at Mount Vernon.[34]

One of Washington's spyglasses, possibly carried for him during military campaigns by William Lee.

Hercules

Portrait of George Washington's Cook, *attributed to Gilbert Stuart, ca. 1795–97.*

William Birch and Son's engraving of the South East Corner of Third and Market Streets, Philadelphia, *1799, depicts street vendors selling meat and produce—a scene in which it is easy to imagine Hercules taking part.*

The Thyssen-Bornemisza Museum in Madrid, Spain, possesses a mysterious portrait of a black man wearing a stylish white jacket, ruffled jabot, and a chef's toque. He stares proudly at the viewer, eyebrows slightly raised, a hint of a smile on his lips. The painting has been attributed to Gilbert Stuart, the artist whose likeness of a grim, stiff-jawed George Washington adorns the dollar bill. The current title of the portrait is *George Washington's Cook.* Many believe this to be Hercules, who served as chef during Washington's presidency. How did Washington's enslaved cook come to have a portrait hanging in a Spanish museum? We do not have the answer, but what we do know about Hercules would make such an enduring legacy unsurprising.[35]

Hercules arrived at Mount Vernon as a teenager in 1767, when George Washington purchased him from a neighbor, John Posey. The young man

Hercules may have used this heavy garden roller to flatten gravel pathways after being sent back to Mount Vernon in 1796.

soon became one of the estate's cooks. By 1777 he had married Alice, a seamstress and dower slave later described as "lame."[36] In September 1787 Hercules was issued three bottles of rum "to bury his wife."[37] These may have been provisions to share with other mourners at a funeral. Alice's death left Hercules with three young children: Richmond, Eve, and Delia.

In 1790, after a hired white cook proved incompetent, Washington requested that Hercules travel to Philadelphia to prepare meals for the executive household. Hercules insisted on bringing thirteen-year-old Richmond to serve as a scullion, or kitchen assistant.[38]

From the kitchen of the president's house, Hercules cooked for the Washington family, friends, members of Congress, and foreign dignitaries. He became a well-known figure in the city, for both his culinary talents and his charismatic personality. As a perquisite of his position, Hercules was permitted to sell kitchen "leftovers," such as bones, feathers, ash, and fat, which were often used for industrial purposes in the eighteenth century. His earnings allowed him to purchase fashionable attire ordinarily unavailable to the enslaved. Years later, George Washington Parke Custis recalled the cook's daily "evening promenade" through the streets of Philadelphia, wearing his finest clothing and greeting friends "with a formal and respectful bow."[39]

Hercules was one of the enslaved people whom Washington rotated out of Philadelphia in order to evade the 1780 Pennsylvania emancipation law. Though Washington asked his secretary to conceal the purpose of the out-of-state trips, Hercules apparently discovered why he was suddenly being sent back to Mount Vernon. In early June 1791 Tobias Lear reported to Washington that the cook "was mortified to the last degree to think that a suspicion could be entertained of his fidelity or attachment to you. And so much did the poor fellow's feelings appear to be touched that it left no doubt of his sincerity."[40] Was the cook's affront genuine? Or simply an effort to cultivate his master's trust?

In late 1796 Hercules was sent back to Mount Vernon permanently and assigned to digging ditches, crushing gravel, making bricks, and weeding the garden. Washington, who was preparing to move back to Virginia after his retirement, may have decided he no longer needed the cook's services in Philadelphia. At Mount Vernon, Hercules may have been assigned to manual labor because no one was there to cook for—or possibly as punishment. In early November of that year, his son Richmond had been discovered stealing a visitor's saddle bags. Washington suspected that Hercules had encouraged his son's theft as part of a plot to take "a journey together." He instructed his plantation manager to "make a watch" of father and son, keeping it quiet lest they should get wind of his suspicions.[41]

This watch proved ineffective. On February 22, 1797—Washington's sixty-fifth birthday—Hercules ran away, alone, from Mount Vernon.[42] Washington made several unsuccessful efforts to locate his former cook, who he believed had escaped to Philadelphia, but Hercules was never found. He may have used connections in Philadelphia's Quaker and free black communities to hide. Or perhaps he traveled farther afield. Before landing at the museum in Madrid, the enigmatic portrait hung at an English estate. Did Hercules capitalize on his culinary skills to be hired by an English nobleman who brought him back across the Atlantic? The mystery continues.

After their father's escape, Richmond and his sisters Eve and Delia remained enslaved at Mount Vernon. A visitor to the estate in March 1797 recalled asking one of Hercules's daughters if she was saddened by her father's disappearance. "Oh! sir," she replied, "I am very glad, because he is free now."[43]

The siblings—who belonged to the Custis estate because of their mother's status—were separated in 1802, after Martha Washington's death. Richmond, then twenty-three years old and valued at a very high £120, was inherited by Eliza Parke Custis Law, who lived in Washington, D.C. Eve (twenty years old) and Delia (seventeen) were sent to Woodlawn, the estate of Nelly Parke Custis Lewis, adjacent to Mount Vernon.[44] Their subsequent fates are unknown.

Ona (Oney) Judge Staines

On January 1, 1847, the abolitionist newspaper *The Liberator* published a letter from Reverend Benjamin Chase describing his recent visit with an elderly African American woman near Portsmouth, New Hampshire.[45] The woman, Ona Judge Staines, had fled enslavement at the Washingtons' household fifty years earlier. Staines's account of her dramatic quest for freedom represents a rare moment when the voice of a (former) Mount Vernon slave appears in the historical record.

Ona Judge, often known as Oney, was born at Mount Vernon around 1774. She was the daughter of Betty, an enslaved seamstress living on Mansion House Farm. Based on Oney's last name, her father may have been Andrew Judge, a white English tailor whom Washington hired from 1772 to 1784.[46] Oney was later described as "a light mulatto girl, much freckled" and "almost white."[47] Like many other slaves of mixed-race descent, she received a post in the household: at age ten, she became Martha Washington's personal maid. Like her mother, Oney was skilled at sewing, "the perfect mistress of her needle."[48] Also like her mother, Oney and her younger sister Delphy belonged to the Custis estate, and so would pass to Martha Washington's heirs upon the latter's death.

When George Washington was elected president, fifteen-year-old Oney Judge traveled with seven other enslaved people to the executive residence, first in New York and then in Philadelphia. She was among the slaves whom Washington secretly rotated out of the latter city in order to evade the 1780 Pennsylvania emancipation law. Washington asked his secretary to accomplish this rotation "under pretext that may deceive both them and the Public."[49]

During Washington's presidency, Judge continued her daily work waiting on Martha Washington—helping her bathe and dress, cleaning and mending her clothing, organizing her personal belongings, and anything else her mistress required. But in the bustling capital city of Philadelphia, life was dramatically different for her and the other Mount Vernon slaves. Judge received nominal cash wages from Washington and, on several occasions, money to go see a play, the circus, and the "tumbling feats." Her visible position in the household meant that she received a regular supply of high-quality clothing. Washington's account book notes purchases for her gowns, shoes, stockings, and bonnets.[50] The city's large free black and Quaker abolitionist communities also offered the young woman new ideas, new connections, and new opportunities to escape.

On May 20, 1796, as the Washingtons prepared to return to Mount Vernon for the summer, Oney Judge fled. As she recalled in 1845, "Whilst they were packing up to go to Virginia, I was packing to go, I didn't know where; for I knew that if I went back to Virginia, I should never get my liberty. I had friends among the colored people of Philadelphia, had my things carried there beforehand, and left Washington's house while they were eating dinner."[51]

Two days later, Frederick Kitt—the hired steward at the executive residence—placed an advertisement in the *Philadelphia Gazette and Universal Daily Advertiser* announcing that Oney Judge had "absconded" from the president's house and offering a $10 reward for her recapture. Kitt described the young woman's "very black eyes and bushy black hair," noting that she was "of middle stature, slender, and delicately formed." She had "many changes of good clothes, all sorts," Kitt warned, and might be trying to pass as a free woman, escaping on a ship leaving the port of Philadelphia.[52]

Kitt's advertisement stated that Judge had run off with "no provocation," but her later interview revealed that she had two reasons for running away. First, "she wanted to be free," and second, she had overheard that she would soon be given to Martha Washington's eldest granddaughter, Eliza Parke Custis Law, who was known to have a fierce temper. Judge "was determined," she recalled, "never to be her slave."[53]

Kitt was right about one thing: after leaving the Washingtons' household, Oney Judge secured passage on the *Nancy*, a ship commanded by Captain John Bolles and bound for Portsmouth, New Hampshire. Judge never revealed Bolles's name until after he died, "lest they should punish him for bringing me away."[54]

Meanwhile, George Washington was stewing. Because the young woman was a dower slave and not owned by him, Washington would be responsible for reimbursing the Custis estate were she not recovered. He also faced pressure from Martha, who was distressed at the loss of a maid who, Washington claimed, "was brought up and treated more like a child than a Servant." Apparently unable to comprehend why she would flee, Washington believed that Judge had been "seduced and enticed away" by a Frenchman.[55]

Even in New Hampshire, Judge was not safe. Just a few months after arriving, she was recognized on the street by a friend of Martha's youngest granddaughter, Nelly Parke Custis. Word of the escapee's whereabouts reached George Washington, who enlisted the help of Joseph Whipple, the customs collector in Portsmouth. Whipple found Judge and tried to convince her to board a ship for Philadelphia. Judge replied that she would readily return, but only if the Washingtons promised to free her after their deaths. Otherwise, she said, "she should rather suffer death than return to Slavery & liable to be sold or given to any other person." There was no seduction by a Frenchman, she assured Whipple, but rather "a thirst for compleat freedom … had been her only motive for absconding."[56]

When Washington learned of Judge's request, he was furious. His response to her proposed deal reveals the tension between his stated antislavery principles and the reality of being a slave owner. He fumed to Whipple: "To enter into such a compromise with *her*, as she suggested to *you*, is totally inadmissible … for however well disposed I might be to a gradual abolition, or even to an entire emancipation of that description of People (if the latter was in itself practicable at this moment) it would neither be politic or just to reward *unfaithfulness* with a premature preference; and thereby discontent before hand the minds of all her fellow-servants who by their steady attachments are far more deserving than herself of favor."[57]

Because of the federal Fugitive Slave Law, which Washington had signed in 1793, slave owners retained the legal right to recapture slaves who escaped across state lines, if necessary with force. As president, Washington knew that using violent measures to seize a runaway slave could anger antislavery residents of northern states. He asked Whipple to continue efforts to recapture Judge, but only if it would not "excite a mob or riot" in Portsmouth, where abolitionist sentiments ran high.[58] If Whipple made further attempts to capture her, Judge evaded them. In January 1797 she married Jack Staines, a free black sailor. The couple went on to have three children: Eliza, Will, and Nancy.

In August 1799 Washington made one more attempt to find and recapture Martha's runaway slave. When Martha's nephew Burwell Bassett Jr. traveled to New Hampshire on business, Washington enlisted his help.[59] Bassett successfully located Judge in Portsmouth and tried to persuade her to return, but again she refused. Though Washington had asked Bassett to avoid any methods that were "unpleasant" or "troublesome," Bassett was determined to take the young woman by force. When he announced his plans over dinner at the home of John Langdon, the U.S. senator from New Hampshire, a sympathetic Langdon secretly sent a messenger to warn Judge. With her husband at sea and one-year-old Eliza in her arms, Judge hired a horse and carriage to take her to the home of a friend, a free black woman named Nancy Jack, eight miles from Portsmouth in Greenland, New Hampshire.[60] Bassett returned to Virginia empty-handed.

After Washington's death in December 1799, Judge said, the family "never troubled me any more." She nevertheless remained a fugitive: the Custis estate could legally recapture her and her children at any time.

Portrait miniature of Martha Washington, painted by James Peale, in 1796, the year that Oney Judge departed, to the dismay of her mistress.

Advertisement.

ABSCONDED from the houshold of the President of the United States, ONEY JUDGE, a light mulatto girl, much freckled, with very black eyes and bushy black hair, she is of middle stature, slender, and delicately formed, about 20 years of age.

She has many changes of good clothes, of all sorts, but they are not sufficiently recollected to be described—As there was no suspicion of her going off, nor no provocation to do so, it is not easy to conjecture whither she has gone, or fully, what her design is;— but as she may attempt to escape by water, all masters of vessels are cautioned against admitting her into them, although it is probable she will attempt to pass for a free woman, and has, it is said, wherewithal to pay her passage.

Ten dollars will be paid to any person who will bring her home, if taken in the city, or on board any vessel in the harbour;—and a reasonable additional sum if apprehended at, and brought from a greater distance, and in proportion to the distance.

FREDERICK KITT, Steward.

May 23   d₤₤

When Judge was interviewed in the 1840s, she was still living at Nancy Jack's home in Greenland. Legally considered a "pauper," she received support from Rockingham County. Her husband and three children had predeceased her. Despite these sorrows, she told her interviewer how her life had changed for the better since arriving in New Hampshire: "She says that she never received the least mental or moral instruction, of any kind, while she remained in Washington's family. But, after she came to Portsmouth, she learned to read; and when Elias Smith first preached in Portsmouth, she professes to have been converted to Christianity."[61]

Oney likely never again saw her Mount Vernon family. Her mother, Betty, died in January 1795. In 1802 her younger sister Delphy was inherited by Eliza Parke Custis Law, the fate that Oney had fled to avoid.[62]

Oney Judge's determination to escape slavery eclipsed any regret over leaving. As one interviewer noted: "When asked if she is not sorry she left Washington, as she has labored so much harder since, than before, her reply is, 'No, I am free, and have, I trust been made a child of God by the means.'"[63] Ona Judge Staines died in 1848.

David J. Kennedy's watercolor view of Rickett's Circus, *the first in America. Oney Judge and other enslaved members of the president's household attended performances in 1793, as did the Washingtons.*

Clothing and Personal Adornment

*Examples of decorative buttons excavated by
archaeologists from the cellar below Mount
Vernon's House for Families slave quarter.*

Most of the time, enslaved people had little choice but to wear clothing that identified them as slaves. The types of garments they received from George Washington depended on work assignments. Enslaved domestic servants received more and better-quality clothing than did field-workers. Men working in the house wore three-piece livery suits, stockings, and black leather shoes with buckles. In keeping with a tradition originating with English nobility, Washington ordered custom white-and-red livery at considerable expense, carefully matching the wool fabric and trimmings to the colors of his family's coat of arms. He also directed that enslaved men grow their hair long and pull it back in a queue (ponytail), in the manner of eighteenth-century gentlemen. Enslaved housemaids wore simpler versions of the gowns their mistress owned, made from less expensive materials (such as linen instead of silk).

To save money, Washington limited clothing rations for all other slaves. Enslaved field hands received just one set of clothes each summer and winter, forcing them to wear the same garments nearly every day. Enslaved seamstresses and hired tailors made these items en masse from coarse cloth. The clothing wore out quickly. In 1792 farm manager Anthony Whitting (Whiting) informed Washington that he suspected enslaved workers were stealing old grain sacks to patch holes in their tattered garments. To prevent further incidents he suggested that Washington might obtain "coarse sacking of European Manufacture (which a Negro could not mend his Cloaths with without a discovery)."[64]

When they could, those enslaved at Mount Vernon bought and traded for garments and objects of adornment that expressed their own taste and style. For those who owned little (and, legally, not even themselves) these small personal objects may have carried great meaning. Archaeologists have found beads, buckles, buttons, watch fobs, and cufflinks at sites associated with the enslaved community, especially the House for Families, the primary slave dwelling at Mansion House Farm until 1793. Despite limited resources, slaves were attuned to contemporary fashion: the artifacts found at slave dwelling sites tend to be less costly versions of the high-end items owned by the Washington family.[65]

Giles

Detail of the unidentified enslaved manservant in livery, from Edward Savage's 1798 engraving of The Washington Family.

In November 1790, George Washington enclosed a thin strip of paper in a letter to his secretary Tobias Lear, who was setting up the new presidential household in Philadelphia. On it Washington wrote, "The whole length of this paper is the circumference of Giles cap measured at the bottom and on the inside . . . being the exact Band of the head. . . . To the black line drawn across the paper is the size of Paris's cap."[66]

Giles and Paris were Washington's enslaved postilions, men who rode and guided the horses that pulled his carriage. Washington had noticed that their hats were wearing out and asked Lear to commission two "handsome" new caps, "with fuller and richer tassels at top than the old ones have."[67] These hats formed part of the white-and-red livery suits that Giles and Paris wore as they guided Washington's coach, emblazoned with his coat of arms, through the busy streets of Philadelphia. Made of fine wool and decorated with woven tape (called livery lace), this distinctive uniform immediately identified Giles and Paris—and the other enslaved men who wore it—as the human property of George Washington.

The more senior of the two postilions, Giles first arrived at Mount Vernon in 1765 as the property of Lund Washington, the estate manager and a distant cousin of George Washington. The latter officially purchased Giles in 1771 for £76.[68] Giles's exact age is unknown, but he was at least twenty years old in 1771. Described at various times as a "house servant" and a coachman, Giles was also a trusted messenger, delivering letters to and from his master as far as Philadelphia and Williamsburg (each about 150 miles from Mount Vernon). Washington provided Giles with a small sum to cover his expenses on these multiday solo journeys.

Giles's position meant that he accompanied Washington on several high-profile trips, seeing far more of the country than most slaves. In May 1787 Giles was one of three slaves who traveled with Washington to Philadelphia for the Constitutional Convention. The others were Paris, the younger postilion, and William Lee, Washington's valet. That summer, an observer recorded meeting "his Excellency General Washington taking a ride on horseback, only his coachman Giles with him."[69]

Strip of paper used by George Washington to measure the caps of his enslaved coachmen, Giles and Paris, for use in having new ones made for them.

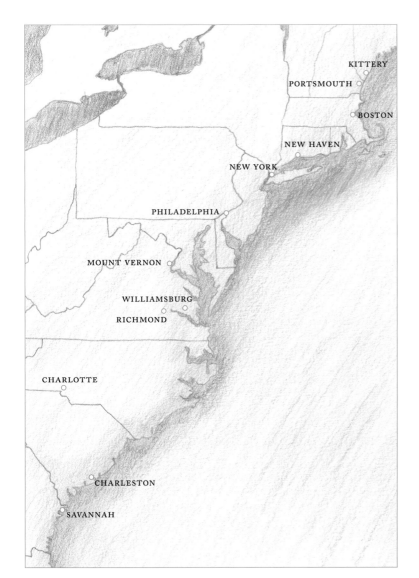

Giles accompanied Washington on his two presidential tours, traveling as far north as Kittery, Maine, and as far south as Savannah, Georgia, in 1789 and 1791.

Giles later returned to Philadelphia, by way of New York, as a postilion in Washington's presidential household. He joined his owner's tour of the southern states in the spring of 1791, driving the baggage wagon. At some point on the trip, Giles suffered an injury or illness that affected his ability to ride a horse. After returning from the trip in June 1791, Washington noted "the incapacity of Giles for a Postilion, who I believe will never be able to mount a horse again for that purpose."[70] Two months later, Martha Washington commented in a letter to her niece, "I am sorry for poor Giles, & fear he never will be well again."[71] Giles does not appear in any of Washington's subsequent letters or accounts.

Daily Life on Mount Vernon's Five Farms

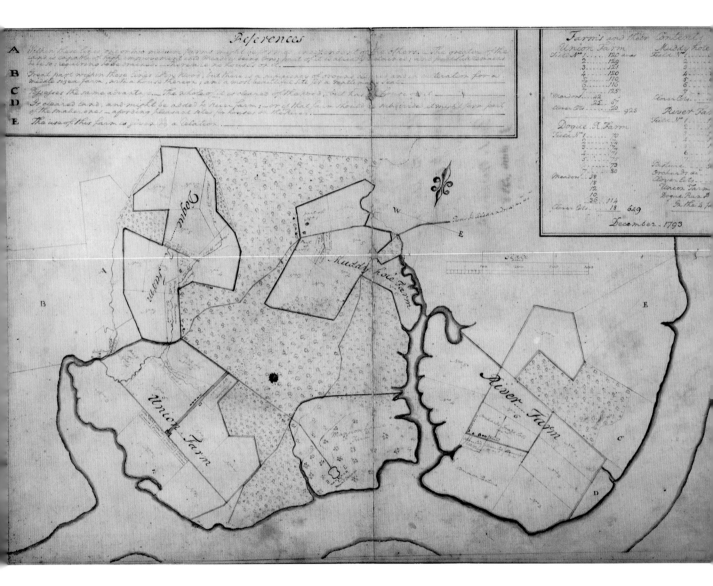

George Washington's 1793 map of Mount Vernon's five farms (clockwise, from center bottom): Mansion House, Union, Dogue Run, Muddy Hole, and River.

Labor defined the daily lives of enslaved people on Mount Vernon's five farms. Under the close supervision of George Washington and his managers and overseers, they worked from dawn to dusk, and often longer, to keep the estate's many operations running. Enslaved people had little control over their schedules or tasks. They lived where they worked, which often meant being separated from family members. Washington provided rations of food, clothing, and blankets, but these were often insufficient for the physical demands of their lives. Indeed, the material world of slavery was largely defined by deprivation. As master, Washington was reliant on slave labor and wielded ultimate control over the lives of the enslaved. He often expressed suspicion that slaves were stealing time or materials and punished them when he believed it was necessary.

Despite their bondage, the men, women, and children enslaved at Mount Vernon found ways to carve out lives for themselves. In the face of inescapable hardship, they demonstrated resilience, resistance, and creativity. Enslaved people grew vegetables and hunted wild game to eat and sell. They mastered skills and could take pride in their work. Some lobbied their master for changes to rations and labor assignments. They acquired personal possessions and outfitted their dwellings with the few items available to them. They married, unions that Washington recognized even though Virginia law did not. The enslaved community celebrated the births of children, nursed the sick, and mourned those who died. They made music and told stories. They defied the law to participate in religious worship and social gatherings. And they fought back by working slowly, breaking and stealing tools, and running away.

Most enslaved people at Mount Vernon worked in the fields on Washington's four outlying farms.

Sambo Anderson

In 1876 the *Alexandria Gazette* published the reminiscences of an "old citizen of Fairfax County." The anonymous author described his visits many years earlier to the home of "Uncle Sambo," a former slave of George Washington who still lived at Mount Vernon as a free man.[72] Although written decades later and clearly tinted with the author's nostalgia, the recollections provide a wealth of information about the formerly enslaved man's life and echoes of his voice. By examining this account alongside Washington's records, we can piece together a detailed portrait of Sambo Anderson.[73]

Anderson was one of the few enslaved people at Mount Vernon in 1799 who had been born and captured in Africa. He recalled arriving in the American colonies "five years before Braddock's defeat" (that is, around 1750). The *Gazette* article reported that Anderson was "a genuine Guinea negro and claimed to have come from a Royal family." The accompanying description suggests his African origins: "He was of a bright mahogany color, with high cheek bones, and was stoutly made. His face was tattooed, and he wore in his ears rings which he informed me were made of real Guinea gold."

The records detailing which slave ship carried Anderson and when George Washington purchased him do not survive, but the enslaved man began appearing in Washington's tax records in 1760.[74] Washington also bought one of his shipmates, a man named Simon.[75] The two men were

The chimneypiece carving in Mount Vernon's dining room is attributed to William Bernard Sears, a hired English craftsman, who may have trained Sambo Anderson and the estate's other enslaved carpenters.

among the dozens of enslaved Africans and African Americans whom Washington purchased in the 1750s as he expanded Mount Vernon's operations after taking control of the property.[76]

At Mount Vernon, Anderson worked as a carpenter, one of the many skilled craftsmen and women at the Mansion House Farm. With a team of about four or five other men, he built and repaired plows, carts, wheels, rakes, door and window frames, livestock pens, fishing boats, and coffins, as well as structures like storehouses, barns, and overseers' houses. The enslaved carpenters also labored in the Mansion, sometimes assisting white craftsmen hired by Washington. Anderson recalled proudly that he had been trained by William Bernard Sears, the English craftsman who carved the wooden mantelpiece in Washington's dining room in the fall of 1775. The *Gazette* recounted that Sears "laid out the work there, and Sambo, with his force, did the manual labor."[77]

The quotations attributed to Anderson in the *Gazette* provide a rare glimpse of how those enslaved at Mount Vernon viewed their master. The former slave recalled Washington's keen eye for detail and exacting standards: "At one time, when he was building a corn house at Mount Vernon, [Sambo] had the frame up and was setting the studding at the gable ends, but had not been particular to use his plumb. His master came riding along, and glancing at the building, said, 'Sambo, that studding is not plumb; knock it off and use your plumb, and always do your work correctly.' Sambo told me that he did not believe any man could have told the defect with his naked eye but his master, 'but,' said he, 'his eye was a perfect plumb ball.'" Anderson also described his former owner as "very particular and the most correct man who ever lived." Washington had, at times, borrowed Anderson's small boat, but never without asking permission, and he invariably returned the boat to the same location: "If it happened to be high tide when he took it, and low tide on his return," Anderson noted, "I have known him to drag the boat twenty yards, so as to place it exactly where he took it from."[78]

Anderson may have kept this boat to expedite visits to his family living on Mount Vernon's River Farm, which was separated from Mansion House Farm by Little Hunting Creek. His wife, Agnes, was a field-worker there. By 1799 the couple had six children: Heuky (age seventeen), Cecelia (fourteen), Anderson (eleven), Ralph (nine), Charity (two), and Charles (one), all of whom lived with their mother.[79] Craftsmen like Sambo Anderson typically visited families on Sundays, their only day off, and occasionally at night during the week. In January 1798 the farm manager noted to Washington that Anderson was unable to work for a day because he was "stopped by the Creek being high." Did rising water unexpectedly extend a weeknight visit to his wife and children?[80]

Although he lived separately from his large family, Anderson was enterprising in finding ways to care for them. He hunted birds and raised

Little Hunting Creek separated the Mansion House Farm, where Sambo Anderson lived and worked, from River Farm, where his wife, Agnes, lived with their children. Anderson kept a small boat, which he likely used to cross the creek to visit his family on Sundays and some nights.

Advertisement offering a $20 reward for the return of Ralph Anderson, Sambo's son, in 1810.

chickens to sell to Washington. He also became a skillful bee-keeper, selling at least fifteen gallons of honey and four pounds of beeswax to his master between 1789 and 1797.[81] Some of this sweetener likely found its way atop Washington's hoecakes, the cornmeal dish the general enjoyed "swimming in butter and honey."[82]

Sambo Anderson was emancipated in 1801 by the terms of Washington's will. His wife and their children belonged to the Custis estate and remained enslaved; they were inherited by Martha (Patty) Parke Custis Peter, one of Martha Washington's granddaughters. As a free man, Anderson settled in a house on Little Hunting Creek, perhaps in or near his family's old cabin at River Farm. To earn money he continued to hunt wild game, selling it to local families and hotels and, as a result, becoming a well-known local figure.[83] After Virginia banned free African Americans from owning firearms without a license in 1806, Anderson applied for and received permission from the Fairfax County Court in 1807 to keep a gun.[84]

Despite their enslavement, Anderson seems to have been able to maintain ties with his family. In May 1810, his son Ralph ran away from one of the Peter family properties in Seneca, Maryland. An advertisement in the *Alexandria Gazette* offered a $20 reward for his return, noting that the twenty-one-year-old had likely escaped to his father, "a free negro man named Sambo, living on Judge [Bushrod] Washington's estate." Ralph's fate is unknown, though his escape was temporarily successful: the same advertisement was published at least forty times in the *Gazette* until December that year.[85]

Anderson later used earnings from his hunting operation to purchase and then free several of his enslaved family members, including his daughter Charity; his grandchildren William and Eliza; and Eliza's children James, William, and John.[86] In 1835, Sambo Anderson and his grandson William were among the twelve former slaves and their descendants who returned to Mount Vernon to assist with the landscaping around Washington's new tomb. When Sambo Anderson died on February 20, 1845, his obituary appeared in the *Alexandria Gazette*. Using an Anglicized version of his name, the brief article noted, "DIED, On the 20th instant, near Mount Vernon, SAMUEL ANDERSON, aged about 100 years, one of the former servants of Gen. Washington, and liberated by that great man in his will. Old Samuel was a native African—had been tattooed in his youth, and bore the marks to the day of his death."[87]

This long-barreled musket, made ca. 1740–50, was especially suited to shooting low-flying birds. Owned by George Washington, it may have been used by Sambo Anderson in hunting fowl that he sold to his master for Mount Vernon's table.

Priscilla

In early July 1798 at Dogue Run Farm, thirty-five-year-old Priscilla gave birth to Christopher, her sixth living child.[88] She did not resume working in the fields until five weeks later. Priscilla's husband and Christopher's father, Joe, was likely unable to see much of his newborn son. Like many enslaved couples at Mount Vernon, Priscilla and Joe lived separately.

George Washington recognized marriages between slaves but nevertheless dictated that work assignments rather than family units determine their living arrangements. Joe worked at the Mansion House Farm as a ditcher and lived in the greenhouse slave quarter during the week.[89]

Replica slave cabin built by Mount Vernon in 2007 (left), based on an early 20th-century photograph of a dwelling on Washington's land that does not survive.

Priscilla was a field-worker and lived with their children in a cabin on Dogue Run Farm. Joe could visit his wife and children on Sundays or holidays. Sometimes Joe may have walked the three miles to Dogue Run after sunset, returning in time for work the next morning. Washington occasionally complained that his enslaved workers were fatigued from this practice of "nightwalking" to visit their families.[90]

As a result of these living arrangements, Priscilla raised her children largely alone, supported by the community at Dogue Run and, as time went on, her older children. When Christopher was born, Priscilla's older children—Sophia (age thirteen), Savary (twelve), Penny (ten), and Israel (nine)—could help their mother with the newborn and two-year-old Isrias.

Priscilla appears to have lost at least one child, possibly two. In a 1792 letter to his farm manager, Washington assured him that, "if proper care and attention has been paid to Cilla's child, it is all that humanity requires."[91] Whether the child had died or was ill is unclear. There is a record in November 1794 of Priscilla giving birth, but Washington's 1799 list of enslaved people does not include a five-year-old child by her.[92] Regular references to Mount Vernon's carpenters making child-sized coffins and the small burial sites located at the slave cemetery reveal the frequency with which the estate's enslaved community bore such losses.

Mount Vernon records indicate that Priscilla tried to flee at least twice. The work report for the week of May 31, 1794, notes that "Silla ran away" for six days. On this occasion, Priscilla was probably pregnant—she gave birth six months later. On October 24, 1796, Washington's farm manager paid £1 to a William Green for "taking up Sillar" (a common spelling of her name).[93] What induced Priscilla to run away while pregnant (on the first occasion) and again just nine months after the birth of her son Isrias (on the second)? Did something happen? Did she intend to return? Did she take any of her children? Was the promise of freedom greater than the pain of leaving her family? Without any records left by Priscilla, answers to these questions remain elusive.

Priscilla and her children lived on Dogue Run Farm, approximately 3 miles from Mansion House Farm, where her husband, Joe, lived and worked as a ditcher.

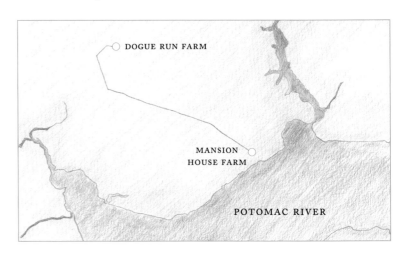

DOGUE RUN FARM

MANSION HOUSE FARM

POTOMAC RIVER

Penny

Priscilla's third daughter, Penny, was eleven years old in 1799. We know relatively little about the lives of enslaved children at Mount Vernon because Washington and his managers did not document their activities in the same way they did enslaved adults. Sometime between ages eleven and fourteen, depending on their physical abilities, enslaved children at Mount Vernon were given formal work assignments. In 1799 Penny's older sisters, Sophia (age fourteen) and Savary (thirteen), joined their mother working in the fields at Dogue Run. Although Penny did not yet have an official assignment, she and other children were expected to perform such simple tasks as fetching water and gathering sticks. She likely also helped care for her three younger siblings while her mother worked in the fields.

In 1801 Priscilla, Penny, and her siblings received their freedom from the provision in George Washington's will. Priscilla's husband, Joe, who belonged to the Custis estate, remained enslaved and was inherited by one of Martha Washington's grandchildren. Priscilla now found herself

Detail from George Washington's 1799 list of enslaved people, including the names of Priscilla and her children.

Benjamin Henry Latrobe's 1796 watercolor depicts two female field-workers wielding hoes, in An Overseer doing his duty near Fredericksburg [Virginia].

responsible for six children and forcibly separated from her husband. In his will, Washington stipulated that children with parents who were "unable or unwilling to provide for them, shall be bound by the Court until they shall arrive at the age of twenty five years." In such cases, he also instructed that the children "be taught to read & write; and be brought up to some useful occupation."[94] We do not know whether Priscilla was forced to use this provision, or if she was able to find the financial security to care for her family. Similarly, we do not know whether Penny and her siblings received the education that Washington desired. Emancipation brought hope for the future, but it did not mean that Priscilla, Penny, and their family were free from the long shadow of slavery.

Kate

On Sunday April 1, 1792, at Mount Vernon's Muddy Hole Farm, an enslaved boy named William felt a sharp pain in his back. Two days later, the twelve-year-old fell ill, becoming "senseless and speechless." The boy's mother, a field-worker named Kate, spent a week caring for him in the family's small cabin. A white doctor was sent for, but on Saturday April 7 William died. The farm manager described the event to Washington, noting that "his death I much regreted because he was a promising Boy."[95] The sorrow of Kate—and her husband, Will, the boy's father—was not recorded.

Two years later Will, an enslaved overseer, approached George Washington with a request. His wife wanted to be the "Granny," or midwife, to the estate's enslaved women. Washington usually paid a white woman to perform this job. Several of Kate's five children were delivered by Susannah Bishop, the wife of one of Washington's hired servants. Kate argued, however, "that she was full as well qualified for this purpose as those into whose hands it was entrusted and to whom [Washington] was paying twelve or 15 pounds a year."[96]

Washington asked his farm manager to look into Kate's credentials and give her the job if she were qualified. There are no surviving records of payments to Kate for attending births, but in 1799 she was given twenty-five cents for the purchase of scissors "to cut the tongues of young children," a reference to fixing tongue-tie, a common oral deformity in infants.[97]

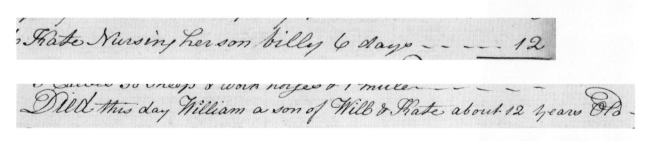

Mount Vernon's manager reported the death of William,
"a promising Boy," in 1792.

Different colors in the soil reveal the tops of graves in Mount Vernon's slave cemetery, including child-sized burials, seen during a 2014 archaeological survey. No human remains are disturbed during this work, which seeks to honor the deceased by locating and marking the burials.

Kate's bold request hints at the social dynamics governing relationships both within the enslaved population and between master and slave. By asking to become the midwife for other enslaved women, Kate ensured that this important role was undertaken by a member of their own community, not an outsider. Her approach to Washington, through her husband's privileged position as overseer, suggests assertiveness and knowledge that Washington would be receptive. Indeed, this incident and others suggest that Washington valued and rewarded competence and skill, even among those he enslaved.

Kate was a common name among enslaved women, so it is difficult to trace her identity. She may be the enslaved woman valued at £30 whom Washington inherited from his elder half-brother Lawrence in 1754.[98] As George Washington's property, Kate and her living children—Molly, Virgin, and Kate—became free in 1801 through the provision in his will. Described as "old" on the 1799 list of enslaved people, Kate would have received clothing and food from Washington's estate for the rest of her life, per the terms of his will. Because her husband, Will, belonged to the Custis estate, he remained enslaved. He was inherited by one of Martha Washington's grandchildren.

Fragment of scissors, excavated archaeologically from the south grove midden at Mount Vernon.

Davy Gray

Davy Gray was about sixteen years old when he first came to Mount Vernon in 1759 as part of Martha Washington's dower share of enslaved workers from the Custis estate.[99] It is unknown whether anyone in his family accompanied him. The young man became a field-worker on several of Washington's farms. As early as 1778 he was supervising other enslaved workers. By 1799 then-fifty-six-year-old Gray was overseer at Muddy Hole Farm, where he lived with his wife, Molly. At various times, Washington also assigned him to oversee the fields of River and Dogue Run Farms. Gray was described as "mulatto," meaning he was mixed race. The origin of his last name is unknown.[100]

Most of Washington's overseers were hired whites from the local region, but a handful of enslaved men rose to this position of authority. For a brief time in the 1780s, three of Mount Vernon's five farms had enslaved overseers. Reporting to Washington's overall plantation manager, the overseers were responsible for supervising day-to-day operations of their fields, ensuring that the enslaved workers performed assigned duties thoroughly and attentively. For those who did not, overseers were also tasked with administering punishment. To his frustration, Washington found that hired workers who met his standards were rare indeed. He chided many overseers for drinking too much, sleeping too late, and neglecting their duties in favor of entertaining friends. By contrast, Gray's work ethic and calm demeanor seem to have met with Washington's approval. In 1793 Washington noted that "Davy at Muddy hole carries on his business as well as the white Overseers, and with more quietness than any of them. With proper directions he will do very well."[101]

As overseer, Gray received certain privileges, such as leather breeches (enslaved field-workers were usually issued clothing of coarse linen), occasional cash gifts, and extra quantities of pork after hogs were slaughtered. He and his wife lived in a house with a brick chimney, sturdier than the standard log cabins with wooden chimneys in which most enslaved field-workers resided.

Davy Gray signed this 1801 receipt with an "X." Few enslaved people had an opportunity to learn to write.

Being an overseer also gave Gray the power to advocate for his fellow workers. In 1793 Washington heard complaints from his slaves that his new method of distributing cornmeal was leaving them with less to eat. Initially skeptical, he changed his mind when Gray assured him "that what his people received was not sufficient, and that . . . several of them would often be without a mouthful for a day, and sometimes . . . two days."[102]

After Washington died in 1799, Gray was among the hired and enslaved workers who were outfitted with mourning clothes for the funeral.[103] Because they were owned by the Custis estate, neither Gray nor his wife was freed by the emancipation provision in Washington's will. On January 12, 1801—just eleven days after the Washington slaves were emancipated—Gray was paid $9.75 for his proportion of 32 turkeys, 20 ducks, and 42 chickens raised for Martha Washington. Gray signed the receipt for this payment with an "X" in place of his name, indicating that despite his position as overseer, he could not write.[104] After Martha Washington's death in 1802, Gray may have been inherited by Nelly Parke Custis Lewis and her husband, Lawrence, who lived at nearby Woodlawn plantation. The fate of Molly, Gray's wife, is unknown.

Modern replica of the 16-sided barn at Dogue Run Farm, where Davy Gray served at times as overseer.

Caesar

On April 14, 1798, plantation manager James Anderson placed a newspaper advertisement seeking an enslaved field-worker who had run away from Mount Vernon's Union Farm.[105] Anderson described Caesar, then in his late forties, as a "black negro" with "a sharp aquiline nose" who stood about five feet seven or eight inches tall and was missing some of his front teeth. The advertisement stated that Caesar usually dressed in homespun black and white, could read and write, and that he "frequently" preached to other blacks in the area. It also noted that Caesar had been seen around Alexandria and at Dr. David Stuart's plantation, "as he has relations at both places."[106]

The search ended on May 7, when George Washington paid an unnamed person $25 for "taking up Caesar."[107] This was not the first time that Caesar had left Mount Vernon without permission. Weekly farm reports note his absence for six days in February 1796, six days in January 1797, and three days in July 1797. It is unclear whether Caesar was captured each time or returned of his own accord. Any punishment he may have received for fleeing also went unrecorded. Although slave literacy was not yet illegal in Virginia, Caesar's ability to read and write was uncommon and likely gave him an advantage, perhaps even allowing him to forge a pass giving him permission to travel.

Caesar's repeated flights to visit relatives hint at the larger network of enslaved people beyond the boundaries of Mount Vernon. Many of the slaves on Washington's estate had been separated from family members and friends when they were bought, sold, or inherited by different owners. The reference to Caesar being spotted at the Stuart plantation makes sense, for many enslaved people belonging to the Custis estate—as Caesar did—lived there. David Stuart was the second husband of Eleanor Calvert Custis, the widow of Martha Washington's son John (Jacky) Parke Custis. Jacky had inherited ownership of his father's land and slaves; as widow, Martha had received life-rights to one-third of the slaves. In 1759, Caesar—between eight and ten years old and valued at £25—was assigned to Martha.[108] It is highly likely that he had relatives and friends among Jacky's share, especially because some of these individuals would have lived at Mount Vernon under George Washington's control until Jacky reached adulthood.

Beyond family ties, enslaved people had other opportunities to interact and forge connections—at the weekly Sunday market in Alexandria, in local stores, on the road while running errands or delivering messages for

This watercolor of The Old Plantation, South Carolina, *attributed to John Rose, ca. 1785–90, suggests the activities that enslaved people enjoyed during their limited "free" time, after sundown, on Sundays, and on certain holidays such as Christmas and Easter.*

their owners, and at social and religious gatherings. Enslaved people required permission to leave their home plantation—or risked reprisal if caught without it—but many did move about the landscape for both sanctioned and covert purposes. About 15 percent of married slaves at Mount Vernon had spouses who lived on another plantation.[109] It is impossible to fully reconstruct this web of associations, but it is clear that, in many cases, Mount Vernon slaves like Caesar were not running *away*—they were running *to*.

The description of Caesar as a minister who preached to local African American communities provides a rare window into the religious lives of enslaved people. We know that eleven of Washington's slaves were baptized at an Anglican church in Williamsburg in the 1760s (whether by their choice or Washington's is unclear).[110] By the 1790s, enslaved people at Mount Vernon had come into contact with Baptists, Methodists, and Quakers who lived in the area.[111] Though we lack the words of enslaved people, we can speculate that religion, heard through Caesar or other ministers, provided comfort as they faced the horrors of bondage.

After Washington died in 1799, Caesar was sent to New Kent, Virginia, to alert Lawrence Lewis, Washington's nephew, and George Washington Parke Custis, his step-grandson, of the death. Caesar received $3 for the journey.[112] Given that he was a proven flight risk, the decision to send Caesar is interesting. After Martha Washington's death in 1802, Caesar may have been inherited by her granddaughter Martha Parke Custis Peter, who lived in Washington, D.C., and later Tudor Place in Georgetown.[113] Caesar may have worked as a field hand at one of the outlying Peter properties in Maryland. Nothing more is known of his life.

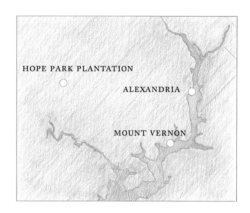

Caesar likely had relatives living about 20 miles west of Mount Vernon, at the Hope Park plantation of David and Eleanor Stuart.

Tom

George Washington's mahogany bottle case, made in London in 1760, had space for twelve one-gallon bottles of liquor.

MOUNT VERNON

SAINT KITTS

Three of George Washington's slaves are known to have been transported for sale in the West Indies.

On July 2, 1766, the schooner *Swift* lay anchored in the Potomac River awaiting a trading voyage to the Caribbean. Below deck, an enslaved man named Tom sat in handcuffs. A foreman on Mount Vernon's River Farm, Tom had been inherited by George Washington from his elder half-brother Lawrence in 1754. Twelve years later, the enslaved man made a failed attempt to flee the plantation. In a letter to Joseph Thompson, captain of the *Swift*, Washington declared Tom a "rogue and a runaway" and directed that he be sold in the West Indies. Washington commented that Tom was "exceedingly healthy, strong, and good at the Hoe," and "he may . . . sell well, if kept clean and trim'd up a little."[114]

Thompson succeeded in selling Tom on the island of Saint Kitts for £40 local currency. In return, Washington received 66 gallons of spirits and 10 pounds of sweetmeats (candied fruit), as well as "two half-joes, 1 pistole," and "small silver" (Portuguese and Spanish currency used in the colonies).[115] Tom was probably purchased by the owner of one of the island's many sugar plantations, known for harsh working conditions and high mortality rates. Nothing is recorded of his life beyond this point.

Washington sold at least two other enslaved people to the Caribbean, his punishment of last resort. In 1772 Will Shag, a thirty-one-year-old field-worker on one of the Custis properties in York County, Virginia, engaged in repeated conflicts with an overseer and twice attempted to run away. Washington paid £13.11s.6d. to a ship captain to transport Shag to Port-au-Prince in exchange for molasses.[116] By the 1780s Washington had stated his opposition to buying and selling slaves, but this did not stop him from selling Jack, a wagon driver, to the West Indies in 1791 "to be disposed of," as a secretary wrote in Washington's ledger.[117]

The threat of such sales loomed over Mount Vernon's enslaved community. When fifteen-year-old Ben was caught fighting and engaging in other "rogueries," Washington instructed his farm manager to tell the young man that if he did not stop, "I will ship him off (as I did Waggoner Jack) for the West Indias, where he will have no opportunity of playing such pranks as he is at present engaged in."[118]

Tom, Will Shag, Jack, and Ben lived in a world in which their bodies were commodities that could be bought, sold, and "disposed of." Being sold to a Caribbean sugar plantation was often akin to a death sentence. Burns, lost limbs, and fatal accidents were common. On average, an enslaved worker was expected to live not more than seven years after arriving in the West Indies.[119]

William Clark's 1823 print of the Interior of a Boiling House, Antigua, *depicts the harsh conditions inside a West Indies sugar mill.*

A pair of iron shackles, 1750–1820. To prevent Tom from escaping again, Washington asked the captain of the Swift *to "keep him handcuffd till you get to Sea."*

George

The week of August 12, 1798, was a sweltering one at Mount Vernon. The mercury of Washington's thermometer flirted with ninety degrees nearly every day. Ominous clouds roiled the sky each afternoon, but fitful rain showers did little to break the heat. Despite the oppressive conditions, business continued as usual among Mount Vernon's enslaved workers, including the three gardeners: George, Harry, and Joseph.[120]

Working under William Spence, an English hired gardener who had arrived at Mount Vernon ten months earlier, the three men toiled in the heat, weeding and planting strawberries in the vineyard enclosure, sowing seeds for spinach and other greens in the kitchen garden, and pruning plantings, harvesting cabbage, and transplanting orange trees in the ornamental upper garden.[121]

George Washington used enslaved labor to make his vision for Mount Vernon's landscape a reality. Among those who performed this labor was a man who shared his master's name. George worked as a ditcher and later a gardener on Mansion House Farm. In the 1780s he was likely among those whom Washington directed to create paths, move and level earth, build walls, sow and cut grass, crush gravel, and transplant groves of trees to realize his plans for an elegant country estate. By the 1790s George was consistently working in Mount Vernon's gardens.

OPPOSITE: *Mount Vernon's picturesque bowling green required extensive skilled labor to create and maintain. Enslaved workers leveled the ground, planted and cut grass, and transplanted and pruned trees.*

An 18th-century copper watering can used by Mount Vernon's enslaved and hired gardeners.

Mount Vernon's upper garden, replanted in
2011 according to the 18th-century layout, with
vegetables surrounded by borders of flowers and
ornamental shrubs.

George first came to Mount Vernon in the 1770s. He was owned by Washington's mother, Mary Ball Washington, who lived in Fredericksburg, Virginia. For a decade, Washington rented him, paying his mother for the use of the young man's labor. While living at Mount Vernon, George married Sall Twine, a field-worker and dower slave at Dogue Run Farm. By 1786 the couple had three children together.

All enslaved people lived with the knowledge that they could be separated from family at any time, but George's position as a rented slave was especially tenuous. In 1787 Washington wrote to his mother that he hoped to stop hiring any of her slaves except for George, who, Washington wrote, "will not, as he has formed connections in this neighborhood, leave it, as experience has proved him I will hire."[122] By this point, Washington's moral qualms made him reluctant to separate enslaved families, and so he acquiesced to George's request.

When she died in 1789, Mary Ball Washington left her "Negroe Boy George" to her eldest son in her will, ensuring that George and Sall's family would stay together, at least temporarily.[123] Proximity was relative, however. Because George was stationed at Mansion House Farm and Sall was a field-worker at Dogue Run, the couple lived apart during the week. George was allowed to visit his wife and children on Sundays.

The couple went on to have seven children: Jesse, Kate, Lawrence, Barbary, Abbay, Hannah, and George. After Washington's death in 1799, the elder George became a free man. His fate is unknown. His oldest daughter, eighteen-year-old Kate, may be the "Kitty" who was valued at £80 and inherited by Nelly Parke Custis Lewis at Woodlawn. Sall Twine and their four youngest children were inherited by Martha Parke Custis Peter and likely sent to one of the Peters' farms in Maryland. Barbary was assigned to work as housemaid at Tudor Place, the Peters' urban residence in Georgetown. According to her family history, she deliberately misbehaved so she could be sent back to the farm—perhaps to see her relatives. Barbary's daughter Hannah later served as a nanny to the Peter children. George and Sall Twine's youngest child, George, may have been among the enslaved laborers stationed at a quarry in Seneca, Maryland, owned by John Parke Custis Peter (Martha Peter's eldest son). In 1847, the quarry supplied red sandstone for the Smithsonian Institution Building, now known as "The Castle."[124]

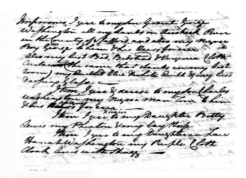

Detail from Mary Ball Washington's 1788 will, bequeathing her "Negroe Boy George" to her son, George Washington.

Epilogue:
Divergent Paths in the Nineteenth Century

Watercolor portrait, Enslaved Girl, *1830, by Mary Anna Randolph Custis, of Arlington House. The unnamed girl may be a descendant of one of the enslaved people inherited from the Custis estate in 1802 by Mary's father, George Washington Parke Custis.*

After feeling conflicted about slavery for the last two decades of his life, George Washington chose to address the issue in his will, drafted in July 1799, five months before he died. In this document, Washington declared that all the enslaved people he owned in his own right would be freed at his wife's death (Martha Washington ultimately freed them earlier, on January 1, 1801). He further ordered his executors to establish a permanent fund to provide clothing and food for those freed slaves too elderly or sick to support themselves. He directed that young children without parents be placed under the guardianship of the court, taught to read and write, and trained in a "useful occupation." He also sternly forbade his executors from selling or transporting out of state any enslaved people before the terms of the manumission went into effect.[125]

Washington knew that these provisions would apply only to those 123 enslaved people he owned directly. The 41 slaves he rented from others would be returned to their owners. The remaining 153 enslaved people, who belonged to the Custis estate, would remain in bondage and be inherited by Martha Washington's four grandchildren after her death, which came in May 1802. Because many Washington slaves had family members owned by the Custis estate, separation from loved ones tainted celebrations of newfound freedom. Even for those who were emancipated, the connection to Mount Vernon and its master continued to have an impact on their lives as they settled in communities nearby.

After Washington's death in December 1799, his heirs brought their own enslaved workers to Mount Vernon. Slavery continued at Washington's home until 1860, when the Mount Vernon Ladies' Association took control of the property. As tourists flocked to Mount Vernon in the nineteenth century, enslaved and free African American workers played a key role in telling the story of George Washington to eager white visitors.[126] Today, investigation into documentary sources, archaeological sites, cultural landscapes, and oral histories allows us to piece together the story of the enslaved community, ensuring that their names and lives are not forgotten.

Tom, an enslaved man inherited from the Custis estate in 1802 by Martha Parke Custis Peter, of Tudor Place in Georgetown. This mid-19th century ambrotype is the only known photograph of a former member of the 18th-century enslaved community at Mount Vernon.

Christopher Sheels

Christopher Sheels was born in 1776, the second child of Alce (likely pronounced "Al-sie"), a spinner at Mansion House Farm. Her other children included Anna, Judy, Viner, Ariana (who died in 1778 as an infant), Emery, Tom, Charles, and Henrietta (or Emenetta). By 1799 Alce had married a free black man named Charles.[127]

In 1789 thirteen-year-old Christopher was among the eight enslaved people taken from Mount Vernon to serve in the presidential household in New York. He likely worked as a waiter. When the capital moved to Philadelphia a year later, he was also among those whom Washington secretly rotated out of Pennsylvania to avoid the 1780 law allowing enslaved people to claim their freedom after six months' residency in the state.

In September 1791, Christopher was sent back to Mount Vernon, where he began working as a carpenter.[128] When Washington and his family returned to Virginia after his second term ended in 1797, Christopher was transferred back to the house and assumed the position of Washington's valet, or personal manservant. As valet, Sheels—like William Lee before him—wore a white-and-red livery suit and looked after Washington's daily needs.

Three incidents in Christopher's life illuminate the complex web of intimacy and dependence, trust and suspicion that characterized the relationship between master and enslaved valet. On October 9, 1797, Christopher was bitten by a rabid dog, possibly Nelly Custis's spaniel,

Men's bunkroom of the reconstructed green-house slave quarter at Mount Vernon, as furnished in 2010. Sheels likely lived here in the 1790s.

Frisk, who later died. Fearing that his valet had been exposed to the disease, Washington decided to send Christopher to William Stoy, a physician who claimed to treat hydrophobia (rabies) with his signature "Stoy's Drops." Stoy lived in Lebanon, Pennsylvania, more than 150 miles away.

In a letter that Christopher presented upon arrival in Lebanon, Washington asked Stoy to "do everything in your power" to heal the young man. "I am particularly anxious for his cure," Washington wrote, "he being my own body servant." Stoy administered his medicine and wrote to Washington that he could "rest assured Christopher is safe."[129] Washington gave Christopher $25 to cover his expenses on the journey; the valet brought back $12.[130] Did Washington's efforts to get medical help for Christopher indicate genuine affection for the young man or simply an effort to protect a valuable investment?

By 1799 Sheels had married a young enslaved woman owned by Colonel Roger West, whose West Grove plantation lay a few miles north of Mount Vernon. Although the marriage was not legal under Virginia law, Washington recognized and approved of the union—until he discovered a note from the woman to Sheels detailing plans to run away together. Found in the yard at Mount Vernon in September 1799, the note revealed that Christopher and his wife hoped to escape in a ship from Alexandria.[131] The young couple's plan was foiled. No other references to this event appear in Washington's papers, so we do not know how it affected Sheels's relationship with his master or whether the young man was punished after the discovery of his plot. If he was, it did not include a demotion: Sheels retained his position as Washington's valet and, presumably, some degree of his master's trust.

OPPOSITE: *The president's house in Philadelphia, depicted in an 1830 lithograph,* Washington's Residence, *by William L. Beton.*

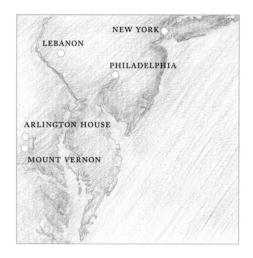

Christopher Sheels traveled 300 miles to and from Lebanon, Pennsylvania, seeking treatment for a suspected rabid dog bite.

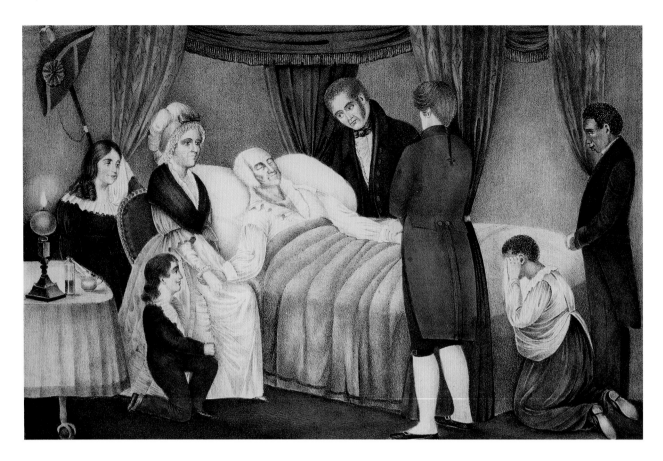

Many versions of The Death of Washington *appeared in the mid-19th century, fifty years after the event. Nathaniel Currier's lithograph shows an enslaved black man and woman at the foot of the bed, identified only as "Domestics."*

Just three months later, on December 14, Sheels stood at Washington's bedside as the retired president battled a throat infection. Washington's secretary Tobias Lear recalled that Christopher stayed with Washington throughout the day. "In the afternoon," Lear recounted, "the General observing that Christopher had been standing at his bed side for a long time—made a motion for him to sit in a chair which stood by the bed side." He sat. When Washington succumbed to his illness late that night, Christopher was one of four enslaved people in the room, along with the housemaids Caroline Branham, Charlotte, and Molly. After his master died, Christopher removed Washington's keys and personal effects from his master's pockets and gave them to a grief-stricken Lear.[132]

Because he belonged to the Custis estate, Sheels was not among the 123 enslaved people freed in Washington's will. Instead, at Martha's death in 1802 he was probably inherited by her grandson, George Washington Parke Custis, who lived at Arlington House. Then about twenty-seven years old, Sheels was valued at the considerable sum of £120. His younger sister Judy was also sent to Arlington House and eventually became a nanny to the children of Custis's daughter Mary and her husband, Robert E. Lee.[133] Their mother, Alce, and other siblings were inherited by Eliza Parke Custis Law. We have no records of Christopher's life after this point.

Kitty

In the first years of the nineteenth century, the enslaved community of Mount Vernon was split apart not once, but twice. When he wrote his will in July 1799, George Washington anticipated the heartache that would arise when he freed the enslaved people belonging to him. Many were married to slaves owned by the Custis estate, whom he did not have the legal power to free. For this reason, he delayed the manumission of his slaves until Martha's death, hoping to lessen the blow to enslaved families whose members had intermarried. "To emancipate them during her life," he wrote, "would, tho' earnestly wished by me, be attended with such insuperable difficulties on account of their intermixture by Marriages with the dower Negroes, as to excite the most painful sensations."[134]

On January 1, 1801, Martha Washington chose to accelerate the emancipation provision, perhaps fearing for her safety in an environment in which the freedom of many depended upon her death.[135] Her action freed about 120 of Mount Vernon's enslaved people, but the Custis slaves (numbering more than 150) remained in bondage. When Martha died just over a year later, the remaining enslaved individuals at Mount Vernon were divided among the Custis heirs.

Kitty, an enslaved milkmaid and spinner at Mansion House Farm, was deeply affected by these transitions. Her husband, Isaac, Mount Vernon's head carpenter, was owned by George Washington and thus received his freedom in 1801. Because Kitty was a dower slave, her nine daughters and seven grandchildren all belonged to the Custis estate and remained enslaved. As a free man, Isaac may have stayed close to Mount Vernon to be near his family.

Fragments of a colonoware bowl, excavated by archaeologists near the Mount Vernon Mansion. This shallow vessel may have been used as a milk pan by Kitty or another dairy maid.

On the list of enslaved people inherited by Eliza Parke Custis Law, the names of "Kitty (milkmaid)" and two of her children, "Barbary" and "Lavinia (Invalid)," appear as nos. 7, 8, and 9.

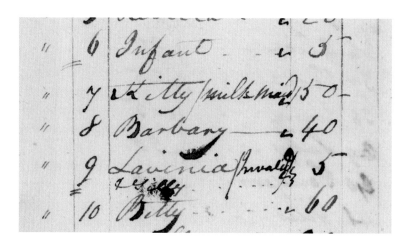

In 1802 the family was separated yet again. At Martha Washington's death, Kitty and her children were dispersed among Martha's four grand-children: Eliza Parke Custis Law, Martha Parke Custis Peter, Nelly Parke Custis Lewis, and George Washington Parke Custis. The grandchildren likely negotiated, selecting the enslaved people they wanted while ensuring that the value of each heir's portion remained comparable. By law, these people were property to be apportioned like any other items in the estate.

The negotiations generated a document with four lists, one for each grandchild.[136] Duplication of common names makes it difficult to assign an identity to each person, but the document nevertheless remains our best source for tracking the fate of Mount Vernon's enslaved community. The four lists give names of enslaved people next to the monetary values assigned to each individual. In most cases, young children were kept with their mothers. Older children and other family members were often split up.

Kitty's family experienced this separation on a large scale, with at least one family member likely going to each of the four Custis grandchildren. The valuations assigned to them by the list maker appear in parentheses. Kitty (£50) and her two youngest children, thirteen-year-old Barbara (£40, listed as "Barbary") and nine-year-old Levina (£5, listed as "Lavinia"), were assigned to Eliza Parke Custis Law, who lived with her husband, Thomas Law, in Washington, D.C. (the Laws would separate in 1804 and later divorce). The description "invalid" next to Levina's name likely accounts for a low monetary valuation. We do not know what injury or illness the young girl had sustained to warrant this designation.

Kitty's eldest daughters, thirty-year-old Sinah (£80) and twenty-eight-year-old Mima (£65), were likely inherited by Nelly Parke Custis Lewis, who with her husband, Lawrence Lewis, built Woodlawn plantation on land formerly part of Mount Vernon. Sinah's five-year-old daughter, Nancy (£30), accompanied her mother, while Sinah's husband, Ben—a miller—was owned by Washington and freed in 1801. Mima was joined by her three young sons, John (£35), Randolph (£20), and Isaac (£6), but not her husband, Godfrey (£100), a carter, who was assigned to Martha Parke Custis Peter's lot.

Three of Kitty and Isaac's daughters were also inherited by Martha Peter, who went on to build Tudor Place in Georgetown: twenty-four-year-old Lucy (£65) and her children Burwell (£25) and Hannah (£15); twenty-year-old Letty (£70) and her daughter Tracy (£12); and eighteen-year-old Nancy (£60).

Grace (£60), twenty-two years old, was apparently the only member of her family to be sent to the estate of George Washington Parke Custis in Arlington, Virginia. Grace's assignment also meant more distant separation from her husband, Juba, who was enslaved at Tobias Lear's Walnut Tree Farm, just upriver from Mount Vernon.

Kitty's third daughter, Alla, does not appear on the 1802 list. In letters and weekly reports from the 1790s, Washington's overseers frequently noted that Alla was ill.[137] She may have died in the three years between Washington's 1799 census and the 1802 division.

After 1802 Kitty and her immediate family lived in five different places, from Washington, D.C., to Virginia. All but one member—her husband, Isaac—remained enslaved. We have no records of their lives after this point. Despite Washington's desire to minimize the "painful sensations" of separating Mount Vernon's enslaved families, those like Kitty's endured them nonetheless.

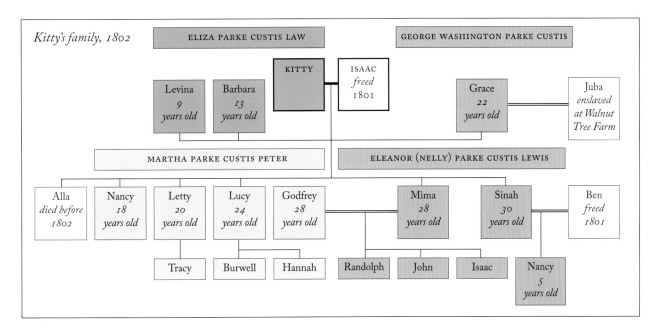

Nancy Carter Quander

Washington's Tomb, *by Augustus Kollner, 1848.*

On November 16, 1835, the *Alexandria Gazette* ran a story about a visit to George Washington's new tomb, which had been constructed at Mount Vernon four years earlier. A reporter on the scene observed, "Eleven colored men were industriously employed in levelling the earth, and turfing around the sepulcher. . . . They stated they were a few of the many slaves freed by General George Washington, and they had offered their services upon this last and melancholy occasion, as the only return in their power to make to the remains of the man who had been more than a father to them; and they should continue their labors as long as anything should be pointed out for them to do. . . . I trust their names will not be forgotten, and that the circumstance here mentioned may be a recommendation to them during life."[138]

Detail from the Fairfax County Register of Free Blacks, showing entry for Nancy Quander's daughter Gracy.

The reporter then recorded their identities: Sambo Anderson, William Anderson, Berkley Clark, William Hayes, Dick Jasper, Morris Jasper, George Lear, William Moss, Joe Richardson, Levi Richardson, Joseph Smith, and Nancy Quander—the only woman—who cooked for the men while they worked.

Nancy was eleven years old in 1799, when George Washington made a list of all the enslaved people on his plantation. She lived on River Farm with her mother, Suckey Bay, a field-worker. Nancy's father, an enslaved man with the last name of Carter, lived at the plantation of Washington's closest neighbor, Abednego Adams.[139] Nancy had two siblings who also lived on River Farm: Rose, who was twenty-eight in 1799, and a four-year-old sister also listed as Nancy on Washington's census. (It is unclear why these two girls have the same name.) Because Suckey Bay belonged to George Washington directly, she and her children were among those freed in January 1801, by Martha Washington, following the provision in her husband's will.

We know only snippets about Nancy's life after freedom. Sometime in the next ten years, she married Charles Quander, a free black man from Maryland. Quander belonged to one of the oldest African American families in the country, descending from a man named Amkwando, who had been captured in present-day Ghana and brought to the American colonies as a slave prior to 1684.[140] Nancy and Charles Quander had three children: Gracy, born about 1811; Elizabeth, born about 1815; and Osmond, born about 1825.

Virginia law required that free African Americans like the Quanders register with local authorities every three years to obtain a certificate of freedom. The burden of proof rested on free people: those who did not have the proper registration could be detained as fugitive slaves. Registration records consisted primarily of name, age, a report of how the individual became free (whether by birth or manumission), and a detailed physical description including skin color, height, build, hair, countenance, and any noticeable scars or marks. The records that survive (covering just a handful of years) are often brief, occasionally error ridden, and always from the perspective of white record keepers. They nevertheless remain a valuable resource for learning about the free black population of nineteenth-century Virginia.

In 1831 the Fairfax County Register of Free Blacks described Nancy's eldest daughter, Gracy, as "a black Girl about twenty years of age five feet and an half inch high prominent cheek bones, pleasant Countenance a scar on the first finger of the left hand." The entry went on to say that Gracy was "the daughter of Nancy a free woman emancipated by Genl. Washington." In 1836 Nancy's daughter Elizabeth—then married to William Hayes—was listed in Alexandria records as "four feet five and a half inches high, about Twenty one years of age of a dark Complexion, a scar on the right Cheek prominent features, considerably marked with the Small pox." Elizabeth's entry also states that she gained her freedom through her mother, who was freed by George Washington.[141]

When Nancy Quander returned to Mount Vernon in 1835 to support the men caring for the tomb, she was joined by her son-in-law William Hayes and her nephew George Lear (son of her sister Rose). Neither of these men had been enslaved at Mount Vernon. In fact, five of the twelve people mentioned in the *Alexandria Gazette* article were the children of former Mount Vernon slaves and had been born free after Washington's death. Their return underlines the deep impact of Mount Vernon on their families' collective memories, even after emancipation.

Many members of the Quander family eventually settled in free black communities near Mount Vernon. One such neighborhood, known as Gum Springs, was founded by West Ford a former slave of Bushrod Washington (nephew of George Washington). Quander family members continue to tell the story of their ancestors and preserve their legacy, as related elsewhere in this volume by Judge Rohulamin Quander and Gloria Tancil Holmes.

Quander Road, in the Spring Bank section of Alexandria, Virginia, runs along land formerly owned by the family.

Edmund Parker

In the summer of 1898, a *Washington Post* reporter visited Edmund Parker on his deathbed. For the previous fifteen years, Parker had worked for the Mount Vernon Ladies' Association (MVLA) as the guard at Washington's tomb. Years earlier, he had been enslaved on the estate. Stricken with stomach cancer, the seventy-one-year-old spoke candidly about his life and journey from slavery to freedom, first as the property of a Washington heir and then in his role as a beloved employee of the historic preservation organization maintaining the estate.

Edmund Parker had arrived at Mount Vernon in 1841, at age fourteen, as one of the enslaved people owned by John Augustine Washington III (known to his family as Augustine). Parker recalled that slavery had been "mighty hard work. Had more put onto me than I could perform, 'cept as I took care of myself. There was mighty heavy timber on that Mount Vernon farm, and we slave folks was pulled and hauled. Altogether, as far as kindness was concerned, I reckon they meant well enough, although life is a burden to a slave person; indeed it is—left without education and the mind terrified all the time."[142]

Parker married Susan, an enslaved woman whom Augustine had purchased for $585 in 1852. Their wedding took place in the library at Mount Vernon and was officiated, unusually, by a white minister. The couple went on to have nineteen children, including two sets of twins.

During the Civil War, Edmund Parker ran away from Mount Vernon, seeking refuge in Union-occupied Alexandria, Virginia, and Washington, D.C., where he cooked for Union troops. In the ensuing years, as a free man, he and his family lived in Alexandria, followed by a stint in Pennsylvania, before finally settling back in Washington.

In 1882 Parker was hired by the MVLA to serve as the watchman at Washington's tomb. Parker thus joined a long line of guards who stood sentry over the pilgrimage site after Washington's new tomb was completed in the 1830s (with the help of former Mount Vernon slaves). Visitors took note of these African American watchmen—first slaves and, later, employees of the MVLA, like Parker. As historian Scott Casper has written, the tomb guards deliberately provided the "authentic" antebellum experience that visitors craved, sometimes claiming a personal relationship with the general (though none had been at Mount Vernon during Washington's lifetime) and crafting engaging narratives "in a dialect that white

Portrait of Edmund Parker, wearing his uniform as guard at Washington's Tomb in the 1880s and 1890s. Mount Vernon superintendent Harrison Howell Dodge drew this portrait for his 1932 memoir.

Sheet music from 1850 for the ballad, Washington's Tomb, *with detail, showing a black man selling souvenir canes to tourists.*

people associated with native black Virginians."[143] One *Washington Post* reporter who visited Mount Vernon many times fondly extolled the estate's timelessness, including "the same old Virginia darky" always stationed at Washington's tomb.[144] Another visitor pronounced, "Old Edmund is a type of the real old time southern negro that is rapidly becoming extinct."[145] Many different men served as tomb guard, but to most tourists, they were an interchangeable and treasured part of the Mount Vernon scenery. Few visitors seemed to realize they were viewing calculated performances, catered specifically to their expectations.

As Mount Vernon became a site of pilgrimage and tourism, African Americans on the estate played key roles in maintaining and interpreting Washington's life and legacy. Some sold souvenir canes made from Mount Vernon trees. Sarah Johnson, Edmund Parker's niece and another former slave of Augustine Washington, worked as a housekeeper and sold milk to tourists for five cents a glass. Her husband, Nathan, worked as "major-domo" in the Mansion, collecting admission tickets, answering questions, and taking and selling visitors' photographs.

Parker and his contemporaries took pride in their work. The dying man recalled fondly the blue uniform with nickel-plated buttons and silver badge that he wore as an employee of the MVLA. Even though visitors seemed to view him as part of the Mount Vernon landscape, Parker's home was in Washington, D.C. He visited his wife, children, and grandchildren every other weekend, staying the rest of the time on a bed in Mount Vernon's old washhouse.

After Parker became ill, the MVLA paid him his monthly wage as a pension, and superintendent Harrison Howell Dodge visited the ailing man. When Parker died on December 30, 1898, his obituary ran in the *Washington Post* and other national newspapers, under the headline, "A Faithful Guardian of Washington's Tomb."[146] The Association paid his funeral expenses and began looking for a replacement. Dodge struggled to find someone "as typical of 'ye olden time'" as Parker, but eventually located a successor.[147] An African American employee stood watch over Washington's tomb until 1965.[148]

Slavery at Mount Vernon: Essays

G.W

Dower

Names	age	Remarks	Names	age	Remarks
River Farm			**River Farm**		
Robin	80	nearly passed Col.d	Ben	70	nearly done Peg for wife
Natt	55	Wife Doll RF don	Breechy	60	not better Ruth his wife
Ned	56	Ditto Hand d° d°	Johny	39	Wife Esther RT don
Ben Cart	22		Richmond	20	No Wife
Peg	58	Husbd old Ben RT don	Ned	20	
Judy	55	Ditto Gunna GW	Henky	17	Son to Agnes RT
Aloe	55	No husband	Jack	22	
Suckey	50	Ditto d°	Esther	40	Husbd Johng d°
Suckey Bay	46	husbd belongs to Adams	Doll	58	Husbd Natt RF GW
Sall	30	Ditto Postn Joe don	Lydia	50	Ditto Smith Geo GW
Rose	28	No husband	Agnes	36	Ditto Sambo Car GW
Penny	20	Husbd Ben Hub GW	Alce	26	Ditto Lears John
Lucy	18	Ditto Cyrus Postn don	Fanny	30	Ditto Alexander
Hannah	12	daughtr Daphne dead	Betty	20	Ditto Lears Reuben
Daniel	15	Son to Suckey RF	Doll	16	No husbd Daught to Doll
Henry	11	Son to Sall d°	Cecelia	14	No husbd Ditto to Agnes
Nancy	11	daught to Bay Suke d°	Jack	12	Son to Doll
Children			Anderson	11	Ditto to Agnes
Elijah	7	Son to Sall RF	Lydia	11	Daughtr to Lydia
Dessie	5	Ditto d° d°	**Children**		
Gutridge	3	Ditto d° d°	Ralph	9	Son to Sall RF
Toby	1	daughtr d° d°	Charity	2	Daughtr d° d°
Hagar	6	d° to Rose d°	Charles	1	Son d° d°
Simon	4	Son d° d°	Davy	6	
Tom	2	d° d° d°	Lewis	4	Cornelia's Child dece don
Joe	1	d° d° d°	Alce	2	
Nancy	1	Daughtr to Bay Suke d°	Suckey	4	Daughtr to Alce RF
Passed Labour			Jude	1	Ditto d° d°
Ruth	70	husbd Breechy don	Milley	1	Daughtr to Betty d°
			Peter	9	Son to Doll d°
			Hannah	old	Cooks Husb God d°

Workers. 17.
Children 9 } together 27.
Passed Col.d 1 }

Workers 19.
Children 10 } making 30
Cook 1 }

Altogether at this Farm 57.

64

Introduction to Part Two

The following essays offer diverse perspectives that provide a broader context for understanding the life stories of the enslaved individuals profiled in Part One. Addressing a question frequently asked by modern visitors to Mount Vernon—What did George Washington think about slavery?—Philip Morgan traces the general's changes of attitude, "from unthinking acceptance to principled opposition," culminating in the manumission provisions of his 1799 will. Mount Vernon historian Mary Thompson, in contrast, chronicles actions taken by the enslaved people—notably, resistance, rebellion, escape—as telling expressions of their viewpoint.

Four essays provide behind-the-scenes glimpses of "how we know what we know" about the estate's eighteenth-century enslaved community, focusing on three broad categories of evidence. Ms. Thompson surveys the many types of documents that have been preserved, and Molly Kerr previews the rich potential of digital technology to draw together thousands of individual references. Eleanor Breen reviews the archaeological evidence, while Esther White turns attention to the plantation landscape.

The last four essays consider the persistent, contested legacies of slavery, in the years since George Washington's death. Scott Casper traces the intertwined history of slavery and freedom at Mount Vernon through the nineteenth century. Maurie McInnis examines well-known paintings from the 1850s, in which northern and southern sympathizers used images of Washington and Mount Vernon to advocate for and against slavery. Turning to the present, descendants of enslaved individuals offer personal reflections. Judge Rohulamin Quander and Gloria Tancil Holmes celebrate the "dynamic and diverse . . . legacies" of descendant families; while recognizing Washington's greatness, they hold him accountable for upholding human bondage. ZSun-nee Matema recalls the emotional moment when she first learned that her ancestor, Caroline Branham, had been an enslaved maid to Martha Washington: "an entire world then opened to me. One rich with the fabric of time and full with the passion of people who lived, worked, and supported the efforts at Mount Vernon."

Page from a list of enslaved people at Mount Vernon, compiled by George Washington in June 1799.

George Washington and Slavery

Philip D. Morgan

By the time Gilbert Stuart painted George Washington in the 1790s, Washington was grappling with how to disentangle himself from the institution of slavery.

George Washington's views on slavery changed radically over his lifetime. When he was a child, hardly any white person questioned the institution of human bondage. To them, it seemed part of the natural order. Owners had no qualms about buying and selling human beings, lashing and branding their "property" like cattle. As he entered adulthood, Washington became further immersed in the slavery system; he and those workers under his control grew ever more entangled. As one historian has noted, Washington "spent more of his lifetime overseeing enslaved laborers than he did supervising soldiers or government officials." The young Virginian experienced no epiphany about the immorality of slavery. Rather, his thinking evolved gradually, painstakingly, and sometimes contradictorily over decades. Washington was no utopian dreamer; he was a realist who came to the decision to free his slaves after years of deep, conflicted reflection. While he never shed completely his earlier attitudes, his thinking was ultimately transformed. He came to question the institution, considered it tragically flawed, and wished to extricate himself from its embrace. Over the course of the eighteenth century, Washington journeyed a long way in his views on slavery, from unthinking acceptance to principled opposition.[1]

Washington became a slave owner at a young age, and much of his life was spent building his estate, the most significant component of which consisted of human property. In 1743, at age eleven, he inherited 10 slaves from his recently deceased father and assumed personal control of them in 1750, when he turned eighteen. He added to his original holding via purchase, rental, and, most dramatically, marriage—in 1759, Martha Dandridge Custis, then the richest widow in Virginia, brought 85 enslaved workers, the so-called dower slaves, under his control (but not his ownership). Yet Washington obtained most of his slaves through natural increase, that is, by an excess of births over deaths. The enslaved women at Mount Vernon gave birth to about 300 children during the half century that Washington built his enslaved workforce. At the end of his life, he owned 123 slaves, the dower slaves numbered 153 (one lived off property), and he rented another 41, bringing Mount Vernon's slave population to 317.[2]

In many ways, Washington was a conventional slave owner, albeit one who operated on a scale that few surpassed. By the late 1780s, he was the sixth largest slave owner in Virginia (based on the slaves for whom he paid tax). He was a demanding, exacting, sometimes querulous master. From the first, Washington expected his slaves to work unremittingly, even in their spare time. After buying a black woman named Clio in 1755, he told his manager to employ her "leizure hour's" in making clothes. From his perspective, his slaves should labor diligently, conscientiously, and, to use one of his favorite words, "steadily." He was a stickler for details, incessantly carping and cajoling. Often exasperated, he frequently complained that his slaves shirked work, that they were careless, deceitful malingerers who engaged in thievery or "atrocious villainies." For him, slaves were "a Species of Property," and he sought to act toward them in a businesslike manner. He fed them the typical corn and hogmeat (or fish) rations; housed them either communally or in one-room huts; allocated the usual skimpy clothing; and ordered punishments when he deemed necessary. He pursued fugitives doggedly and even shipped three inveterate runaways to the West Indies.[3]

Despite being a stern taskmaster, Washington also played the role of patriarch, buying produce from some of his slaves' gardens, purchasing their teeth possibly for his dentures, allowing slaves to borrow his nets to fish in the Potomac, or handsomely tipping slaves when visiting other plantations in Virginia. As head of an extended family, Washington thought of his enslaved workforce as his "people," part of his household, not a dreaded internal enemy. He recognized their families and sought to avoid separating them. He acknowledged their skills; a quarter of the adults on his farms were tradesmen, individuals who had mastered a craft. From 1766 onward he employed slaves as overseers, and at one point three of his five farms were under black supervision. Of Davy Gray, one of his black overseers, Washington said that he performed "as well as the white

Overseers, and with more quietness than any of them." In addition, Washington sometimes used black folk healers to minister to the health of his slaves. In short, black individuals could earn his respect.[4]

It is difficult to pinpoint when Washington began to have doubts about slavery, but the origins of his initial misgivings were inherently pragmatic. Perhaps the first crucial turning point came with his decision to abandon the cultivation of tobacco. In 1763 he reduced the size of his tobacco crop, and by 1766 he had largely stopped growing it altogether. From then on, he was committed to becoming a farmer and no longer a planter. Mixed farming could be accomplished with slaves, but grains required much less labor to grow than tobacco. Washington found himself grappling with a fundamental problem: he had too many slaves. Whatever opposition to slavery was then emerging in his mind, it was almost entirely economic.[5]

If the first shifts in Washington's views on slavery were largely practical and self-interested, the glimmerings of his ideological opposition to slavery would have to wait until the Revolutionary era. While Washington was serving in the House of Burgesses in 1772, the lawmakers petitioned for a ban on the slave trade, calling it a practice of "great inhumanity." Virginians could afford to take such a stance because of natural increase among their slaves; two years later, in a meeting chaired by Washington, freeholders from Fairfax County strongly opposed the importation of slaves as "wicked, cruel and unnatural." In 1774 Washington declared that British policies, if acceded to, would make Americans "tame and abject Slaves, as the Blacks we Rule over with such arbitrary Sway." Using the language of enslavement, as American revolutionaries were wont to do, inevitably raised the issue of chattel bondage and the tyranny it involved. Indeed, Washington thought young Virginians were becoming "imperious & dissipated from the habit of commanding slaves."[6]

The Revolutionary War also broadened Washington's thinking about the capacities of black people. Exceptional individuals impressed him favorably. The loyalty shown by his body servant William (Billy) Lee, who accompanied him throughout the war, was such that Washington would later single him out in his will for immediate emancipation. In 1775 Phillis Wheatley, a young black poet, sent the general a poem inspired, as she put it, by "the fame of your virtues," prompting him to praise her for its "striking proof" of her "great poetical Talents." When he arrived in Massachusetts to head the Continental Army, Washington held the conventional slave owner's conviction that slaves should never be armed in large numbers. But before long, military exigencies, the valor of black troops, and the opinions of members of his personal staff who were idealistic about black military abilities—among them the Marquis de Lafayette, Alexander Hamilton, and John Laurens—caused him to change his mind, although he remained forever cautious about plans to arm slaves. Just after approving an all-black Rhode Island battalion in

Portrait of Phillis Wheatley by an unidentified artist, after Scipio Moorhead, published in Wheatley's book, Poems, *in London in 1773.*

1778, he announced to his manager that he longed to "get clear of" or "quit" slavery.[7]

In the mid-1780s, Washington's view that slavery needed to be abolished took firmer shape. Like many of his contemporaries, as well as the writers of the abolitionist tracts he read, Washington thought abolition should be gradual, "by slow, sure, & imperceptible degrees." He declared that "there is not a man living who wishes more sincerely than I do, to see a plan adopted" for the abolition of slavery, and he insisted that it must be done by legislative authority. Whatever the inspiration—whether the individual manumission plan proposed by Lafayette, the hectoring of religious figures such as the Quakers, abolitionist tracts, moral doubts, concern for personal and national reputation, or a sense that slavery was an economic anachronism—Washington was on record, albeit privately, endorsing the abolition of slavery.[8]

The next decade, when Washington was president, saw his last sustained attempts (before the drafting of his will) to extricate himself from the "peculiar institution." He posited various schemes: leasing some of his farms to "substantial farmers" who might hire his freed laborers; selling his western lands and using the resulting funds to finance in whole or in part the freedom of some of his slaves; hiring out slaves to earn income that would free others. He hoped to manumit both the slaves he owned and Martha's dower slaves. These projects foundered because of his inability to rent or sell his western lands, the reluctance of the Custis heirs to embrace his plans, and the intractable problem of how to minimize family separations if the Washington and Custis slaves, who had intermarried, could not be freed at the same time.[9]

Washington came a remarkably long way from the boy who unthinkingly ruled over slaves, the young master who took for granted the laboring system of his birthplace, and the mature owner who ruthlessly sold off fugitives. But mastery was hard to relinquish. Strains of his earlier behavior and reasoning persisted to the very end, evident in his dogged pursuit of fugitives such as Oney Judge and Hercules. Indeed, although he was the only prominent founding father to free his slaves, he did so contingent upon the death of his wife—his mastery thus did not end in his lifetime. In one final twist of fate, Martha, apparently fearful of her life at the hands of slaves eager for her to die, freed her husband's slaves on January 1, 1801. Washington never had a high opinion of black people, but he seems not to have thought of them as inherently inferior. He believed that education—as reflected in a progressive provision of his will directed at enslaved children—and hard work could overcome the deleterious effects of slavery. Ultimately, he held a more optimistic view of a post-slavery future than did Thomas Jefferson. In an irony of ironies, the rock-solid realist of Mount Vernon was more visionary than the idealistic dreamer of Monticello.[10]

One of seventeen pamphlets that Washington owned on the subjects of slavery and abolition.

Resisting Enslavement:
"The Roguest People about the House"

Mary V. Thompson

Virtually all of the documentation about slavery at Mount Vernon comes from the pens of white observers, whether members of the Washington or Custis families, hired farm managers, or visitors to the estate. As a result, the thoughts and voices of the enslaved—rarely heard directly—are especially valuable. In lieu of the written word, the actions of enslaved people can speak volumes about not only their reactions to the institution of slavery but also the actions of those trying to control them.

Methods used by enslaved people at Mount Vernon to rebel against their situation ran the gamut of behaviors documented elsewhere in late eighteenth-century Virginia.[1] Some practices were especially successful because they were impossible to prove. For example, feigning illness carried far less risk than other forms of resistance. Again and again, and with increasing skepticism, Washington asked his farm managers to explain various illnesses among the enslaved workforce. In 1794 he noticed from the weekly reports that Sam had "not done a days work since I left Mount Vernon" three months earlier. He ordered his manager to look into the case but not to contact a doctor, "for [Sam] had Doctors enough already, of all colours and sexes, and to no effect." Washington believed the principal problem, supposedly "an Asthmatical complaint," was in fact "pretense" and "Laziness." If Washington was correct, Sam's ploy apparently was effective. His owner complained that he "never could be got to work more than half his time."[2]

Even harder to prove, and probably used more often, were the methods of procrastination and production of careless work. These could lead to fairly immediate rewards when the expected amount and quality of work were lowered. George Washington eventually came to the conclusion that the majority of his slaves were genuinely clumsy and incapable of performing better. Several times, when faced with opportunities to improve agricultural operations with new inventions, he declined because of reservations about his slaves' abilities. In 1793 Washington expressed his doubts about the practicality of an English threshing machine "among careless Negros and ignorant Overseers." He thought it might prove useful were it fairly simple in construction, but warned that "if there is any thing complex in the machinery it will be no longer in use than a mush-room is in existence."[3]

Many tasks could be slowed down or spoiled. In 1795 Washington characterized Mount Vernon's enslaved carpenters as an "idle set of Ras-cals" who could take an entire week to construct a chicken coop, contrary to evidence of their skill at building. He wrote from Philadelphia that it would take his estate carpenters "a month, or more" to construct "buildings that are run up here in two or three days (with not more hands)."[4]

Other efforts to foil productivity (and increase costs to the owner) in-cluded misplacing equipment. Sometimes the act was as simple as dropping a tool in the field. Washington complained to one manager that "nothing hurts me more than to find . . . the tools and implements laying wherever they were last used, exposed to injuries from Rain, sun, &ca." In the fall of 1792, Washington directed that "all the Tools [be] collected from the scattered situation in which they are, and all that are not in use, put se-curely away." As he reminded another manager, loss or damage of the tools, "though nothing to the Overseers," was a great expense to him.[5]

More aggressive acts of resistance carried greater risk of detection and punishment. One of the actions most frequently mentioned in Washing-ton's papers is theft. The many references to stealing, and the many kinds of objects stolen, convey a virtual siege mentality that was developing on the part of the master and his family, who seem unable to overcome the larcenies occurring around them.[6] In a largely preindustrial society, even seemingly petty losses could be significant. When it took anywhere from three to nine months to fill orders for goods from abroad, any manufac-tured item was likely to be expensive and hard to replace.

Although the slaves at Mount Vernon were suspected at various times of arson and sabotage, and some people on the estate feared that slaves

The storehouse on Mansion House Farm, where tools and materials were distributed to enslaved workers.

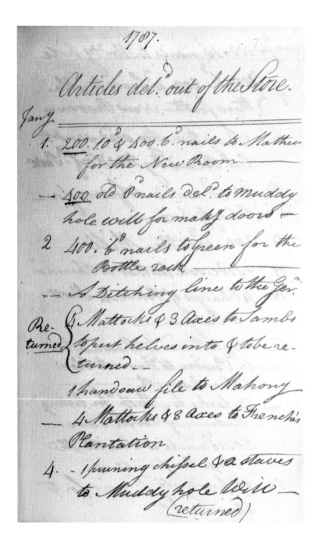

A January 1787 entry in the Mount Vernon Store Book records the distribution of nails, a handsaw file, mattocks (a kind of pickax), and other items.

would try to poison them, no proven instances of such actions occurred in the eighteenth century. A storage building for corn went up in flames in March 1787, leading Washington to surmise that the cause of the blaze was "either by carelessness or design." While he thought that the "latter seems most likely," he noted that "whom to suspect was not known."[7] In the mid-1780s, Washington hired an elderly English farmer named James Bloxham to provide agricultural advice and help him manage the estate. Possibly because of his age, Bloxham had difficulty adjusting to life in Virginia. At one point, he wrote to a former employer that he would probably be leaving America when his contract was up. He confessed that he did not like the slaves and was afraid that he was "Rather in Danger of being posind [*sic*] among them."[8]

Perhaps the most emphatic means of resistance used by slaves was to run away. This action was often a response to problems with an owner or overseer, both in general and at Mount Vernon, but it could also be a positive act whereby a person took advantage of an opportunity to break away, settle in a new location, and start life anew as a free man or woman. Escaping slavery was not without tremendous personal cost, however, because it meant breaking all ties with family and friends left behind. The logistics of being accompanied by children or elderly relatives prevented many women from escaping and meant that more men than women attempted to run away.[9]

The most atypical escape from Mount Vernon happened in the spring of 1781 when 17 individuals (14 men and 3 women) took advantage of the arrival of a British warship in the Potomac to make a bid for freedom. Six years earlier the royal governor of Virginia, John Murray, fourth Earl of Dunmore, had issued a "much dreaded proclamation" offering "Freedom to All Indented Servts & Slaves (the Property of Rebels) that will repair to his majestys Standard—being able to bear Arms."[10] The 17 self-liberators made their way to the British frigate *Savage*, probably in what was described as "a very valuable boat" over twenty feet long. Seven of those who escaped (5 men and 2 women) from Mount Vernon were returned sometime after the siege at Yorktown in the fall of 1781. An unknown number may have died of disease during the war, while still others are known to have left with the British to make new homes in Canada and Sierra Leone.[11]

Enslaved persons with skills or trades to support themselves and who were familiar with both white society and the English language had the best chance of escape. Those who fit this description were frequently artisans or personal servants in close contact with their owner and his family; they therefore had more opportunities than field-workers to interact and become comfortable with the world beyond the African American community in the quarters. The type of work also made it more likely that these individuals would develop closer emotional ties with the white family, and they were often given special privileges. The sense of betrayal when such a slave escaped could be strong.

At least three freedom seekers who attempted to leave the Washingtons matched this profile—Christopher Sheels, Oney Judge, and Hercules—and the latter two succeeded. The experiences of Oney Judge and Hercules illustrate an especially significant aspect of slave resistance. None of the privileges and advantages they received was enough to outweigh their desire for freedom. All were willing to give up the emotional support of family and friends and a life of relative material comfort (compared to the lives of most enslaved Africans) in order to risk physical punishment and possible demotion if caught, as well as considerable insecurity if successful, in the hope of ultimately gaining control over their own lives.

"Anxious for the Weekly Remarks": Documenting Slavery at Mount Vernon

Mary V. Thompson

When I began working at Mount Vernon in 1980, I was fresh out of graduate school. Much of my coursework had been spent reading about and discussing the development and practice of slavery in colonial America and, more particularly, in Virginia. Research on this topic had been ongoing in the academic world for about thirty years, so I was surprised to find slavery little discussed at Mount Vernon—or any other historic house. By 1990 I was given the go-ahead to begin researching slavery at this estate, but I continued to encounter colleagues who said, time after time, that there was simply not much to be found in the surviving records.

Contrary to those skeptics, Mount Vernon has been uniquely blessed and burdened by the wealth of information left by George Washington and those who knew him. Where many historic houses have virtually no documentation from which to work, Mount Vernon has almost too much. For a historian studying slavery at this site, the many types of sources must be painstakingly sifted to extract bits of information. These sources include not only George Washington's own voluminous writings (both diaries and correspondence, which are projected to include ninety volumes when publication is completed), but also Martha Washington's correspondence, financial ledgers and account books, runaway ads in newspapers, weekly reports from managers and overseers, descriptions left by visitors to the plantation in the eighteenth and nineteenth centuries, and reminiscences by family members and former slaves, to name only a sampling of the available documents.[1] Pictorial sources—drawings, paintings, portraits, and photographs—can be particularly important in rendering the world of two hundred years ago real to modern audiences, who live in an increasingly visual world. Similar sources from other plantations can put the Mount Vernon slaves and their experiences into context, a vital part of understanding how typical or atypical those experiences might have been. The space here is too limited to explore what we can learn from each type of source, but a closer look at what, at first, seems like rather dry material—lists—can reveal much of interest.

Members of the Washington and Custis families prepared slave lists for a variety of purposes throughout the eighteenth century. There are lists documenting the names of enslaved individuals inherited by George Washington after the deaths of his father and older half-brother Lawrence, in 1743 and 1752, respectively.[2] Other lists provide names of people owned by Martha Washington's first husband, Daniel Parke Custis, and show how these individuals were dispersed after he died unexpectedly in 1757, before writing a will. There are lists showing who among the Custis slaves were sent to Mount Vernon in 1759, when Daniel's twenty-seven-year-old widow, Martha Dandridge Custis, married George Washington, and who arrived over a decade later.[3] George Washington also kept detailed financial records, which reveal that he purchased more than 60 slaves during the twenty-one years prior to the start of the American Revolution.[4] Taken together, these lists and financial records tell the story of how the enslaved community at Mount Vernon came into being.

George Washington composed this list in July 1799, noting the names, ages, and skills of the people he rented from his neighbor, Mrs. Penelope French.

A similar source, known as titheables lists, was drawn up each year by Washington for tax purposes.[5] On them he recorded the names of each man—black or white—and each black woman of working age, as well as the farm on which they lived. In addition, he noted some of the job specialities they held (overseers, house servants, and artisans are identified). From these lists we know that in 1761 Mount Vernon was worked by 62 individuals, divided into the following categories: 6 hired or indentured white men; 10 enslaved domestics (4 men, 6 women); 9 enslaved male craftsmen; and 37 enslaved field-workers (21 men, 16 women). Thirteen years later, there were 15 hired or indentured white men; 15 enslaved domestics (6 men, 9 women); 13 enslaved male craftsmen; and 91 enslaved field-workers (49 men, 42 women).[6] The titheables lists thus document the growth of, and changes to, the Mount Vernon labor pool, along with the ways in which Washington was moving people among farms to balance out his workforce, in the years before the Revolutionary War.

Still other lists are valuable for determining the range of experience for a given population at a specific time, or even through time. Particularly illuminating are two lists drawn up by Washington for his own use: the first in 1786, as he struggled to reacquaint himself with the enslaved community after the war, and the second in 1799, thirteen years later, as he made preparations for the division of his estate after his death.[7] Where the titheables lists enumerate only slaves of working age, these two documents provide information on gender, age, occupation, and family relationships for all the enslaved people under his control—essential data for people researching their ancestors. Looking at the 1799 list, we see that of the 96 married slaves at Mount Vernon, only 36 lived in the same household as their spouse and children. Another 38 were married to people who, because of work assignments, were living on one of Washington's other farms, while 22 had spouses who either belonged to other plantation owners or were free. These figures suggest that enslaved individuals were picking their own spouses and had both the freedom of movement and the ability to meet and socialize across plantation boundaries, necessary for getting to know potential mates. A comparison of these two slave lists allows us to draw inferences about emotional aspects of enslaved life at Mount Vernon, for example, the importance of having multigenerational families on the plantation or the fact that large segments of the population lived on the same farm for more than a decade. The resulting sense of stability may have helped mitigate some of the many uncertainties that were a basic feature of life in slavery.

Much of the documentation on slavery at Mount Vernon exists as a result of Washington's extended absences from the plantation he so dearly loved. In all, he was gone from the estate for about twenty years of his life. While away, he typically kept track of events through correspondence with his farm managers, reminding one such worker at the time of the Constitutional Convention that he was "anxious for the weekly remarks."[8] After the Revolution, he required written reports even when he was home. These documents provide tremendous detail about the workings of the plantation, ranging from the makeup of the workforce on each farm (how many men, women, boys, and girls were employed) to how many person-days were devoted to specific tasks, how much time was lost to illness, and exactly what kinds of ailments were afflicting the enslaved community.[9]

Washington also kept meticulous financial records, logging both major purchases from abroad and small out-of-pocket expenses. In addition to documenting the purchase of slaves, these records tell of clothing and other items that were bought for specific slaves, as well as the myriad ways enslaved people acquired money—from the practice of tipping domestic slaves during visits to friends, to enslaved individuals selling produce from their gardens to neighborhood residents as well as to the master and mistress of Mount Vernon.

Filling out the picture presented by these financial papers are Martha Washington's letters and instructions to family members and servants (hired, indentured, and enslaved), inventories and wills, and descriptions of the plantation, as well as of individual slaves, that were recorded by guests to Mount Vernon. Visitors were in an interesting position. Generally of the same social status as the Washingtons, they were often, especially after the Revolution, from outside the American South. Slavery was unfamiliar to many of them, and thankfully several took time to talk to enslaved people and record impressions of their lives or their own words. Because most of those enslaved at Mount Vernon could not read or write, and so left no records of their thoughts and feelings, the few times when their voices can be heard, even when filtered through the words of an observer, are invaluable.[10]

Some of the individuals and families from Mount Vernon can be traced well into the nineteenth century. Accounts kept by Washington's executors show that his estate continued to care for the elderly slaves he freed through his will—providing wood, clothing, food, medical care, and, in the end, coffins—until the mid-1830s, by which time all had died. Research into the correspondence and other papers from the Washington and Custis families, as well as newspaper articles, federal census records, and the registrations required for all free black people in the jurisdictions around Mount Vernon, provides physical descriptions of individuals, gives clues to the growth of families after they left the estate, and shows at least some of them becoming landowners by the next generation.[11]

The story of the enslaved community at Mount Vernon is a rich one, made possible by the generations of people who safeguarded such an ephemeral thing as papers—not just letters written by George and Martha Washington, but the wide variety of documents described above. This story could not have been told without them, even if they had no idea that it was "hidden" within.

The Tiniest of Details: A Digital Gateway to Mount Vernon's Enslaved Community

Molly H. Kerr

Statistics on the enslaved population at Mount Vernon, from list compiled by George Washington in June 1799 (detail).

Little, if anything, remains written in the hand of the enslaved people who resided at Mount Vernon during George Washington's lifetime, but much can be found written *about* them, hidden in documents usually read for information about the first president and his family. Changing the focus from the Washingtons to more mundane details, such as the provision of clothing or food, illness, or tasks performed on the plantation, reveals a wealth of data about the enslaved community. Mount Vernon has undertaken an ambitious project to collect and catalogue each reference related to the complex population of enslaved individuals associated with George and Martha Washington.[1] Entering the myriad references into a database allows for this information to be compared, synthesized, and analyzed as never before possible.

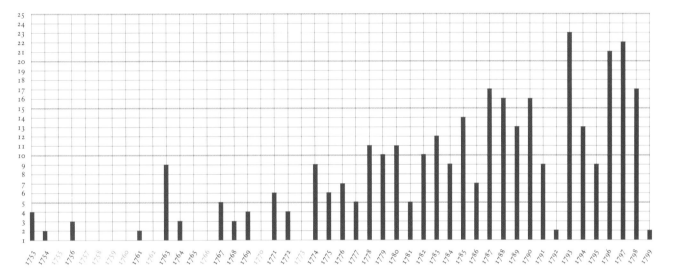

The Mount Vernon slavery database originated as a way to connect the artifacts found in the excavations of the slave quarter known as the House for Families with the people who may have lived there by searching the written record for more information about their daily lives.[2] The digital humanities database team began by establishing a baseline community of identified individuals, using names enumerated by George Washington in 1786 and 1799, plus additional names recorded in research reports compiled by Mount Vernon historian Mary V. Thompson.[3] Information on occupations, places of residence, and family associations enabled us to distinguish specific individuals, sorting out multiple people with the same name, or a single person with a name spelled in various ways (such as Breechy, also written Breachey, Bridgey, and Britchy, to name a few).[4] After a year of data entry, we identified more than 500 members of the enslaved community at Mount Vernon. The names Will and Jack are the most prevalent, with at least thirteen each.[5]

These 500 people emerge from the minutiae of more than 28,000 entries, with data broken out across more than 80 fields. To focus on daily

This chart illustrates the number of recorded childbirths (342) in the enslaved community at Mount Vernon between 1753 and 1799. Records of childbirths were found in ledger accounts for payments to midwives and weekly farm reports that indicated a woman was in childbed.

life, each database entry is defined as an "event," incorporating information on *who* (including name, gender, family relationships), *where* (including both location and movement on the landscape), and *why* (what triggered the reference to an enslaved individual, such as provisioning, skills, or payments made for goods or services). The straightforward references name specific individuals: "To Overseer Morris pr [per] order Mrs Washington 3 … o … o."[6] More challenging are the references to actions that clearly involve, but do not name, enslaved persons: "Cut and secured all my Wheat (by Stacking) at River & Creek Quarters—abt. [about] 60 Acres. Carpenters, Smiths, & home Gang employd [employed]."[7]

The story of Morris provides a solid example of the utility of the database in identifying and telling the story of both an individual and the enslaved community. On May 13, 1795, the enslaved carpenter Isaac received sixty 10-penny nails to construct a coffin for "Old Morace."[8] The database contains more than 150 records of individuals named Morris. Using the "who, where, why" model, we assigned each record a unique name (e.g., Morris A, Morris B), telling them apart based on when a specific event happened and where it took place, among other facts. The records reveal at least two men named Morris at Mount Vernon and two on Custis properties elsewhere. Looking at the records assigned to these men, it becomes clear that the Morris who died in May 1795 is the Morris who belonged to the Custis estate and who had been brought to Mount Vernon from New Kent County, Virginia, early in the Washingtons' marriage, when he was less than thirty years old and valued at £60.[9] This Morris worked as a carpenter until 1766, when he was made overseer at Dogue Run Farm, thus becoming one of several enslaved men who rose to this position. Hannah, identified as Morris's wife in 1799, moved in 1766 from Muddy Hole to Dogue Run Farm; George Washington had purchased her and her child for £80 in 1759.[10] Through the years, we can trace Morris receiving suits of clothes, leather breeches, shoes, shirts, hog meat, rum, and money (often given around Christmastime "for encouragement").[11]

Although little is explicitly recorded about Morris's activities as a carpenter, cataloguing events for which no names were assigned can provide additional clues. Many of Washington's documents refer simply to "my Carpenters." Analyzing who was known to be at a particular place at a specific time sometimes enables names to be identified. Thus, a search for events associated with the skill of carpentry between 1760 and 1766 suggests that Morris may have been sent to a neighboring farm to work on John Posey's barn in 1761 and that he likely helped harvest wheat in 1763 and 1764, when the estate's carpenters assisted with the harvest.[12] The following year, 1765, the carpenters constructed a schooner.[13] Although none of these records mention Morris by name, as one of the carpenters he likely assisted with these tasks. Perhaps his performance during harvest and boat construction encouraged Washington to convey to Morris the responsibilities of overseer.

By using the database to access all possible records simultaneously, we can learn much about Morris and other enslaved residents at Mount Vernon. The project presently focuses on eighteenth-century documents, but we plan to expand into the nineteenth century to explore individuals' lives up to emancipation, both those freed by Washington's will and those who remained enslaved by descendants of the Custis family. Eventually, we hope to circle back to ways in which the documents can be connected to the material culture identified through archaeology and Mount Vernon's museum collections. The analytic power of modern technology enables new research possibilities, as tens of thousands of artifacts and lines of text provide the tiniest of details. When brought together in a single place, these details tell a rich story—the collective biography of the enslaved community at Mount Vernon.

The Archaeology of Enslavement: Mount Vernon's House for Families

Eleanor Breen

The only view of the House for Families slave quarter, in Edward Savage's painting of the East Front of Mount Vernon, *ca. 1787–92 (detail).*

"We entered one of the huts of the Blacks, for one can not call them by the name of houses. They are more miserable than the most miserable of the cottages of our peasants. The husband and wife sleep on a mean pallet, the children on the ground; a very bad fireplace, some utensils for cooking, but in the middle of this poverty some cups and a teapot."

With the exception of this quote from a Polish visitor to Mount Vernon plantation in 1798, written documents tell us very little about the interiors of dwellings for enslaved people and, therefore, very little about their personal lives—physical conditions, culinary traditions, customs, cultures.[1] Inside the quarters within these "spaces of blackness," members of the enslaved community constructed lives beyond the labor that consumed most of each day's waking hours.[2]

Over the past fifty years, the buried remains of slave dwellings throughout the American South have emerged as key sources of evidence for telling a more diverse and inclusive story of plantation life in the eighteenth century.[3] At Mount Vernon, an estate-wide survey in 1984 identified more than thirty archaeological sites, including the House for Families slave quarter, which was located at the end of the row of outbuildings along the north lane, adjacent to the upper garden. Until about 1792 this slave quarter (named the House for Families on a 1787 drawing by Samuel Vaughan) was the primary dwelling for enslaved people assigned to the farm that encompassed the Mansion and outbuildings. It was then torn down to make way for a new slave quarter, contained in two low wings attached to either end of the brick greenhouse.

In 1985, archaeologists excavating the House for Families site discovered a partially intact six-by-six-foot brick-lined cellar filled with nearly three feet of trash dating from 1759 through 1792, discarded by the en-

Interior of greenhouse slave quarter, as installed in 2010.

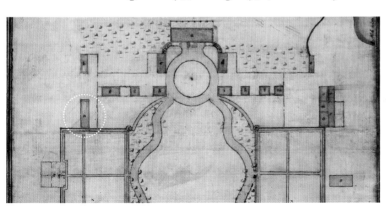

Location of the House for Families slave quarter at the north end of the upper garden, in Samuel Vaughan's 1787 drawing of Mount Vernon's grounds (detail).

slaved individuals living in the large building above.[4] Excavation of this one site dramatically enriched the interpretation of African American history, both at George Washington's home plantation and beyond. The artifacts used and discarded in the cellar offered an unprecedented glimpse into the living spaces above.[5]

Since the artifact assemblage from the House for Families cellar was unearthed thirty years ago, the archaeology of enslavement has matured as a discipline, allowing scholars to ask new questions and make new discoveries about a community whose private lives received meager historical note, particularly in the areas of foodways and personal possessions.

Perhaps the most important discovery generated from the initial analysis of the House for Families artifact assemblage in the 1990s was a revised understanding of Afro-Virginian foodways at Mount Vernon. These findings demonstrated conclusively that enslaved people played a significant role in the subsistence economy, hunting, trapping, and raising a variety of animals to supplement the insufficient and monotonous rations issued by Washington (which generally consisted of cornmeal, salted pork, and some fish). Zooarchaeologists (specialists in analyzing animal bones) studied the 80,000 bones and identified 55 species, including wild game like deer, squirrel, turkey, and blue crab, as well as domestic animals such as cows, pigs, sheep, and chickens. Identification of 18 fish species suggests that slaves likely also supplemented and diversified the provisions of shad and herring allotted to them from Washington's extensive fishery enterprises. Finally, the preservation in the cellar trash of gunflint and about 600 pieces of lead shot (in a variety of sizes) supports the hypothesis that slaves used firearms to hunt for wild game.[6] This finding has become less surprising and even commonplace as additional slave quarter sites

Fragment of white stoneware excavated by archaeologists at the House for Families site (left), with an intact plate of the same pattern.

have been excavated. When the initial study of the mammal and fish bones was completed in 1993, it was the largest and most significant collection of slave-related faunal material unearthed.[7] Archaeological research at other sites of enslavement in ensuing years has revealed that the diets of residents in the House for Families fit into a broader pattern of foodways, one dominated by pork and beef (and sheep, to a lesser extent) and supplemented by domestic fowl and wild species.[8]

Recent research has also expanded the story of Afro-Virginian foodways at Mount Vernon beyond meat and fish to include fruits, vegetables, and other foodstuffs. Archaeobotanists specializing in plant remains have identified 33 different types of seeds, nutshells, and field crop remains. These include 249 specimens of carbonized seeds, primarily edible, fleshy fruits like persimmon, with lesser amounts of peach and cherry. Mount Vernon slaves could have foraged for persimmons, a sweet and slightly tangy fruit that ripens after a hard frost, usually in November, from abundant native trees. Most of the preserved nut remains had fallen from black walnut trees, again a common species on Mount Vernon's landscape. These sweet, oily, and nourishing nuts represented a source of protein during fall harvest periods. In addition to foraging for available foodstuffs, Washington allowed slaves to spend nonwork hours tending small gardens. The remains of beans and peas suggest these plants were a common sight in the plots.[9] Comparative botanical analysis has shown that enslaved people throughout Virginia experienced the need to supplement provisions with nuts, fruits, and vegetables from personal gardens and the surrounding landscape.[10]

Broken ceramics from the House for Families assemblage provide another important data point. Fragments of white, salt-glazed stoneware plates decorated with a molded rim pattern (known as dot, diaper, and basket) were most likely part of a large table service that included 72 plates received by Washington from England in September 1757. Contrary to expectations, Mount Vernon archaeologists have found relatively few fragments of these stoneware plates in a large midden, or trash deposit, dating to the pre–Revolutionary War period, despite its location close to the kitchen and main house (where the wares would have been in continual use until 1769; at that date, a newer, more fashionable table service arrived). Instead, the large number of sherds found in the House for Families cellar suggests that the stoneware plates from 1757 were handed down to the people living in the quarter.[11]

Nor were plates the only kind of hand-me-downs that passed from big house to quarter. On three occasions in the 1760s and 1770s, Washington ordered wineglasses in the latest fashion and was sent sets of enameled wineglasses.[12] Archaeologists found four of these glasses in the House for Families cellar deposit and none in the midden near the kitchen and main house. These "special provisions" bestowed upon en-

Colonoware bowl, archaeologically excavated at Mount Vernon's south grove midden, near the kitchen and main house.

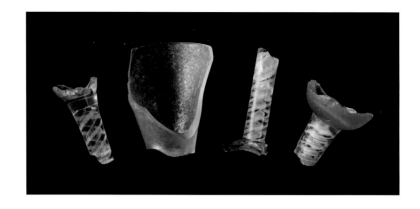

Fragments of wine glass stems excavated at the House for Families site.

slaved people living and working close to the Washingtons afforded material benefits that slaves on outlying farms did not receive.[13] Such benefits must be balanced against the disadvantages incurred by living near the white household: constant supervision, limited privacy, and the "on call" nature of the work undertaken by many of the Mansion slaves living in the House for Families.

Archaeologists studying artifacts from sites associated with slavery have begun to expand the story of access to commonly unearthed items—for example, ceramics, beads, buttons, buckles, straight pins, and wine bottles. Store ledgers and plantation accounts make clear that, although some Virginia slaves received special provisions like plates directly from their masters' households, they were also able to purchase their own using cash or barter. As early as 1757, Washington paid enslaved laborers for potatoes, a practice that continued through the 1790s with other foodstuffs such as honey, chickens, eggs, ducks, melons, and beans.[14] How did enslaved people spend this hard-earned money? One cheap and readily available item was buttons.

In the decades before the Revolutionary War, Washington purchased some 8,000 buttons. This quantity suggests that many of the 49 buttons found in the House for Families assemblage were provisioned, with the exception of one type: linked buttons, or what we would call cufflinks. Only once prior to the Revolution is Washington documented as purchasing a pair of linked buttons, relatively expensive and gold plated ones, presumably for himself.[15] In the House for Families cellar, however, we find a variety of partially intact linked buttons, which we can hypothesize were purchased from a local store (see p. 24). Because these buttons were interchangeable and not fixed to clothing, as were shirt or waistcoat buttons, they offered a degree of personalization and expression of fashion in an otherwise undifferentiated wardrobe.

Enslaved African Americans living at Mount Vernon devised a variety of strategies to acquire the artifacts found in the House for Families cellar—by hunting, fishing, gardening, foraging, receiving special provisions, bartering, and purchasing. Certainly trade and theft account for the presence of some items as well. But what did slaves make for themselves that helped them negotiate the daily demands of labor or small pleasures of private life? Archaeologists hypothesize that enslaved people produced colonoware, a low-fired, locally produced, unglazed ceramic. This craft tradition drew from a mix of African, Native American, and European potting traditions. Though occurring typically as a relatively small proportion of the overall ceramic assemblage, colonoware appears to be a staple of the foodways process on eighteenth-century quarter sites, including at Mount Vernon. The House for Families yielded 42 sherds representing 6 vessels of colonoware, or 8 percent of the total ceramic assemblage. In contrast, the midden near the kitchen and main house contained the largest assemblage of colonoware found thus far by archaeologists at Mount Vernon. There, 915 colonoware sherds represent 27 vessels, or 14 percent of the ceramics in the pre–Revolutionary War phases of the midden site. This finding reveals that at Mount Vernon colonoware was a staple not just of African American foodways but of the plantation as a whole.[16] Vessel forms suggest that enslaved cooks ate and cooked from colonoware and used certain shallow, wide dishes as milk pans for collecting and cooling milk in the early dairy nearby. Archaeologists have yet to find evidence that Mount Vernon's enslaved people made these wares on the plantation, so the question remains: What was the source for these nonimported wares, and how did they arrive at Mount Vernon?[17]

Ongoing excavations and analyses continue to reveal insights into the enslaved community at Mount Vernon. Excavations in the unmarked slave cemetery near Washington's tomb call attention to enslaved and free black people who lived and died at the plantation, in a way that few sites can. Despite the volumes of papers and letters that Washington kept, we know little about the history of the sacred wooded area. The cemetery is not mentioned during his lifetime, raising a question of when the woods started to be used as a burial ground. Discovering basic information, including how many burials exist, where they are located, and how the cemetery is arranged, offers tribute to the deceased. Through hand excavation to expose the tops of the holes dug to place a burial, as well as the use of ground-penetrating radar, we can decipher the interments of adults and children and determine that the graves face east, a common Christian and African tradition.[18] A single artifact has been identified that connects the cemetery to the House for Families quarter: two fragments of nearly identical linked buttons, one found at each site.

We may never know the names of the people who wore these buttons or the names of those buried in the cemetery, but the enslaved community at Mount Vernon left behind material traces that provide meaning, texture, and understanding of their lives, discoverable only through archaeology.

Fragments from matching linked buttons, archaeologically excavated at Mount Vernon's slave cemetery (top) and House for Families site (bottom).

The Landscape of Enslavement: His Space, Their Places

Esther C. White

In 1760 Anthony, Mount Vernon's miller, conducted an experiment with George Washington to determine why the plantation's gristmill was not more efficient. As Washington wrote in his diary, "old Anthony attributed [the problem] to the low head of Water (but Whether it was so or not I cant say—her Works all decayd and out of Order wich I rather take to be the cause)."[1] The two men held different thoughts about the problem, and Washington recorded both hypotheses without a hint that his science partner was a slave belonging to the Custis estate. Old Anthony had arrived at Mount Vernon in April 1759, part of a group of enslaved people that the widowed Martha Dandridge Custis brought with her from the Virginia Tidewater when she married Washington.[2] Only a year later, Anthony's analysis of the mill's elevation suggested the depth of his understanding of his new surroundings.

Plantation landscapes are a primary source for investigating enslaved communities and should be approached with the same level of inquiry that we apply to text and objects. Washington's brief diary entry indicates that Anthony's knowledge of the terrain around the mill was different from, and perhaps more finely honed than, his own. Similarly, other enslaved people understood and perceived landscapes in ways that were separate from the views of their white masters.

One way to think about the cultural landscape of enslavement is through the contrast between space and place. Enslavers, such as George Washington and other plantation owners, controlled spaces; they dictated to the enslaved where to live and work, and they provided a minimum of resources with which to survive and construct lives. Enslaved people transformed these spaces into places: homes, yards, gardens, fences, trails, and many other adaptations that were outgrowths of their lives.[3] Such modifications held meanings that were different from, and often invisible to, the ruling class. The spaces that Washington saw, and the places that the enslaved community created, are revealed through an examination of two maps of the Mount Vernon plantation and a plan of the Mansion House Farm, the core of Washington's enterprise.

Old Anthony was moved to Mount Vernon when Washington was

Archaeological survey reveals outlines of burial shafts at Mount Vernon's slave cemetery, 2014.

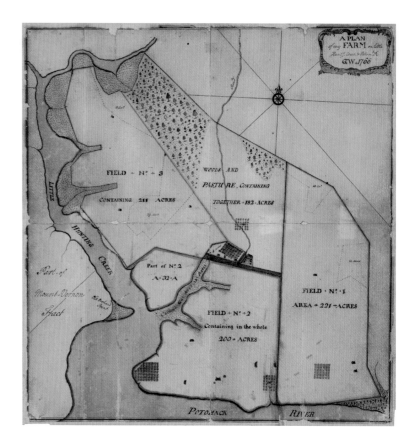

George Washington's 1766 "Plan of my farm on Little Huntg. Crk. & Potomk. R." indicates a variety of houses and agricultural buildings in different sizes and styles.

just starting out as a tobacco planter, and we have little knowledge of the tobacco landscape in existence when he arrived. A survey drawn by Washington a few years later, in 1766, provides our earliest glimpse of what became River Farm, with twenty-two buildings spread around the area.[4] Houses of various sizes with chimneys are set on the edges of fields and next to or within several orchards. Other structures, without chimneys, are probably tobacco barns and agricultural buildings. Some rectangles suggest garden plots. There is a cacophony of building shapes, sizes, and styles as well as a random scattering of structures across the landscape (a randomness not seen on later maps of the plantation). This drawing represents the best depiction we have of the places created by Mount Vernon's enslaved tobacco cultivators.

A second map, drawn by Washington in 1793, shows his later wheat plantation with great order and precision, characteristics suggesting his military experience as well as his adoption of new agriculture practices after the Revolutionary War (p. 28).[5] This map shows five farms, Washington's managerial division of his property; at the core of each farm, Washington depicted small houses, indicating slave quarters. The quarters at Union and River Farms are placed neatly at the edges of cleared fields, along roads with nearby overseers' houses, providing a means for constant surveillance.

Comparison of the 1793 map with written descriptions of each farm and Washington's correspondence with plantation managers strongly suggests that his illustration is an idealized representation of space rather than a careful survey of places. Washington wrote to his farm manager in 1791: "The Houses at the Ferry and French's Plantations are to be removed to the center of both … as soon as circumstances will admit of it."[6]

Details from George Washington's 1793 map of his five farms show slave quarters at Union (left) and River Farms (right) tightly grouped alongside roads, with larger overseers' houses nearby (see page 28 for full map).

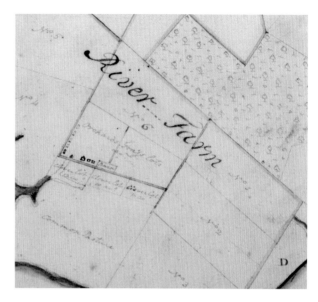

This job had not yet been carried out in December 1793 (after he had created the map), and he further instructed that the quarters at River Farm be placed in "some uniform shape in a convenient place."[7] The desired reorganizations were evidently slow to occur; as late as 1795 Washington inquired, "Are the Cabbins at River and Union farms all removed, as were intended?"[8]

The multiyear endeavor to reorganize these two farms provides important clues about the places. Although Washington illustrated and described all the quarters identically, his inquiries in 1793 imply that at least two different sizes of houses were present, requiring different methods to move. He asked his manager if the larger ones, called quarters, could be moved "on Rollers, or after taking them to pieces," whereas the smaller ones, called cabins, he "presume[d] the people with a little assistance of Carts can do themselves."[9] The former dwellings are believed to have housed two families, and the latter were smaller homes for single families; both were constructed of logs.[10] More importantly, since the slaves lived in "houses of their own building," it is probable that variations existed in size, layout, construction, and other details, according to the skills, resources, needs, and personalities of builders and occupants, details lost to Washington as he drew boxes on his map.[11] Washington depicted the areas surrounding the fields, farm yards, and quarters as wild wooded

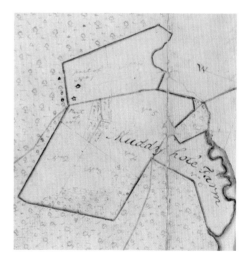

Slave quarters at Muddy Hole Farm are not arranged as rigidly as at the other farms, in Washington's map of 1793 (detail).

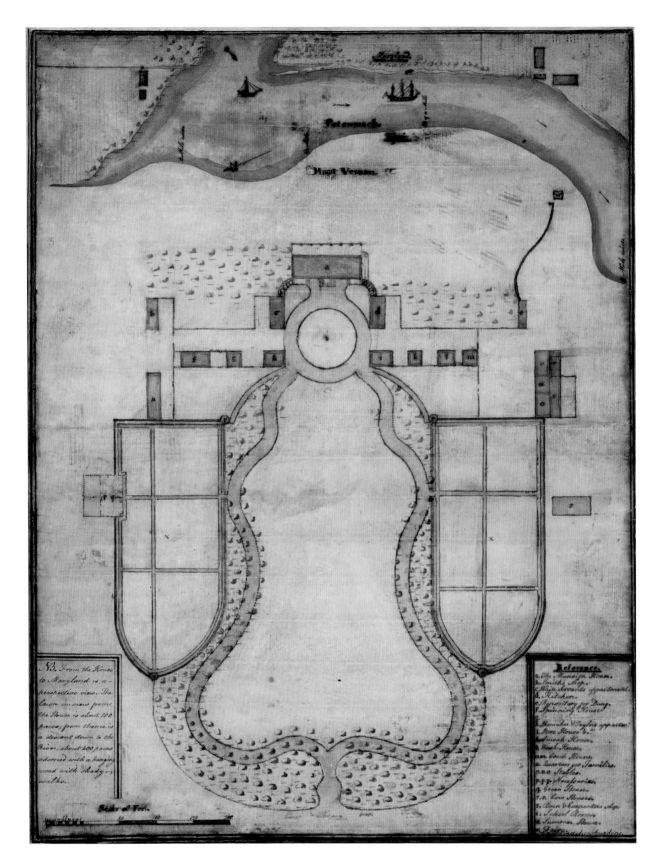

spaces, rather than the complex patchworks of gardens, yards, fences, animal enclosures, trails, footbridges, and dozens of other features that undoubtedly existed on this vast landscape where hundreds of people lived.

In contrast to the neat lines of the quarters at Union and River Farms, those at Muddy Hole Farm show three buildings in a wooded area and two buildings in a field. This is probably the earlier arrangement of dwellings, which Washington did not attempt to regularize. His reluctance to order the layout of Muddy Hole as rigidly as that of Union or River Farm could be related to his relationship with the enslaved overseer at Muddy Hole. Davy Gray had served successfully as overseer for several years, and Washington clearly held him in respect, writing that he "carries on his business as well as the white Overseers, and with more quietness."[12] Perhaps the two men's mutual history was a factor in keeping the older layout.[13]

Although we have no maps drawn by Washington of the area immediately surrounding his own residence, Samuel Vaughan, an English visitor, sketched the core of Mount Vernon and then produced a large watercolor that he presented to Washington in 1787.[14] Vaughan's drawings illustrate the formal landscape, which was still under construction at the time of his visit. Begun in 1775, creation of this landscape was a major undertaking accomplished by the labor of dozens of enslaved ditchers and laborers. To transform the area around the Mansion, they hauled and leveled the bowling green; demolished and built new buildings, walls, roads, and fences; and planted hundreds of trees, bushes, and vegetables. Vaughan's drawings present this landscape as manicured and exact, and the presence of a scale suggests that his are precise renderings of the core of Washington's plantation. In thanking Vaughan for the gift, Washington praised the drawing's accuracy of the "houses, walks, shrubs" and merely corrected Vaughan's omission of the willow mounds at the bowling green gate, the "only departure from the orig[ina]l."[15]

Other sources—visitor accounts and Washington's letters—suggest that the lives of more than eighty people in residence left a greater presence on this formal landscape than is evident from Vaughan's precise illustration. An unknown number of cabins were located across the north lane, where slaves tended their own chickens and gardens, taking advantage of the proximity to their owner to sell him chickens and eggs. Enslaved children were forbidden to play in sight of the Mansion because of Washington's belief that they damaged the plantings and marred the scene.[16]

Such clues hint at a vibrant and active place, one filled with life in ways that neither Vaughan's drawings nor Washington's maps reveal. Reading these images of the landscape in conjunction with other primary sources, we can begin to discern complex and nuanced meanings—the spaces that Washington knew were really the places the enslaved community called home.

Samuel Vaughan's 1787 drawing (detail) depicts the formal arrangement of bowling green, curving pathways, and walled gardens as the core of the landscape leading up to the Mansion. A neat line of outbuildings extends out on each side of the Mansion circle, leading on the left to Quarter or House for Families at the end of the upper garden. The slave cabins that were located on the north lane are not shown.

Slavery and Freedom at Nineteenth-Century Mount Vernon

Scott E. Casper

At least eight African Americans, probably slaves of John Augustine Washington III, standing outside the Mansion in 1858.

Slavery persisted at Mount Vernon for six decades after George and Martha Washington died. General Washington's enslaved women, men, and children received their freedom by the terms of his will, and Mrs. Washington's dower slaves were sent to her grandchildren's homes and plantations. The nineteenth-century history of slavery at Mount Vernon is therefore the story of people who never belonged to or worked for the "Father of His Country." Between 1802 and 1860 Washington's heirs assembled and dispersed two new populations of enslaved African Americans. In the eyes of visitors, these people continued to work for George Washington's memory: telling stories of "the General," tending the grounds he once trod, or simply embodying the hospitality associated with earlier times. At the same time, African Americans formed their own communities and families on this hallowed ground. Mount Vernon's identities as slaveholding Virginia plantation and national patriotic shrine came into conflict at moments when the fundamental fact of American slavery—the commodification of human beings—became starkest.

For the nineteenth century, the basic facts of slaves' lives are documented in texts that owners and officials deployed to establish and enumerate legal holdings, such as censuses, slave lists, wills, and estate records. These sources permit historians to trace family connections across generations and between Washington family plantations in Virginia's Jefferson and Fauquier Counties as well as at Mount Vernon. More revealing are the letters, diaries, and farm books of later Washington family owners; unpublished accounts written by visitors; and newspaper and magazine articles describing sojourns at Mount Vernon. In these sources we find husbands and wives, parents and children, and extended kin networks constructing and reconstructing families in slavery and later in freedom; laboring people performing and sometimes resisting their work; and, especially at Mount Vernon, African Americans both narrating and representing a historic past that white visitors sought to experience.[1]

Approximately ninety enslaved people lived and worked at Mount Vernon under Bushrod Washington, George's nephew and an associate justice of the Supreme Court, who inherited both the Mansion House Farm and Union Farm. Many arrived between 1802 and 1815, members of families whom Bushrod had inherited from his father, John Augustine (Jack) Washington I. They included Oliver Smith (1760–ca. 1835), Bushrod's "waiting man," as well as Oliver's wife, Doll (b. ca. 1765), and their nine children. Oliver Smith became renowned for showing visitors the room in which Washington had died, implying or stating that he had been present on that sorrowful day. His son Phil (1790–1846) trained under Mount Vernon's German-born gardener, Johann Ehlers, and subsequently became the estate's principal gardener, tending the greenhouse and plantings and offering (later, selling) cuttings and fruit to visitors. At Union Farm, another extended family included sister Sinah (b. 1761) and brother Ham (b. 1773) and their spouses, children, and grandchildren, nearly thirty in all by 1815.[2]

Bushrod's enslaved people lived among free African Americans. Manumitted by George Washington's will, the aged William (Billy) Lee and others who received pensions from the estate continued to live on the grounds.[3] At least nine of Bushrod's slaves joined the Alexandria Baptist Society, established in 1803, whose members included white people, free black people, and urban slaves. We know relatively little of daily life at Mount Vernon because few records for this period survive (and possibly because Bushrod was less concerned with farm management than his

Bushrod Washington, shown here in a 1783 portrait by Henry Benbridge, inherited Mount Vernon and took up residence after Martha Washington's death.

uncle had been). What is clear is that unrest mounted in the early 1820s, with a series of escape attempts documented by Bushrod's advertisements in the *Alexandria Gazette* from March to June 1821 for the runaways' capture and return.

In August 1821, Bushrod sold fifty-four people, sundering families and making national news. He appears to have sold most of those who lived and worked at Union Farm, including Sinah's and Ham's families, possibly because that farm was increasingly unprofitable. The news broke in a Leesburg, Virginia, newspaper, soon followed by the nationally circulated *Niles' Weekly Register*: Bushrod Washington, nephew of America's founding hero and president of the American Colonization Society, had sold people south, deeper into bondage. He responded to the charges in a Baltimore newspaper, justifying his actions as economically necessary. He claimed to have sold entire families together, on the unenforceable condition that the buyers keep them intact. In an instant, Mount Vernon's enslaved community shrank from nearly ninety (according to the 1820 census) to fewer than forty. Oliver Smith's family remained, but the spring's turmoil continued. Oliver and Doll's twenty-four-year-old daughter Hannah (ca. 1797–1823) was accused of attempting to poison the white manager at Union Farm; she was imprisoned, tried, convicted, and sentenced to death. Although her sentence was commuted to "transportation" out of Virginia, she died in prison before it could be enforced. While she awaited trial, two of her brothers, George (b. ca. 1794) and Ned (b. ca. 1804), ran away; both were captured and returned to Mount Vernon.

The already fractured slave community was divided again after Bushrod died in 1829, this time among his heirs. Oliver and Doll stayed, as did their son Phil, along with Jesse Clark (1785–1848), George Frazier (1808–1844), a young dairymaid named Sarah (b. 1809), and several children. But the Smiths' other four sons, like most of Bushrod's remaining people, fell to other heirs and were taken far from Mount Vernon.

After this dispersal, fewer than a dozen of the enslaved people who had inhabited Mount Vernon in the 1810s and 1820s remained on the Mansion House property, which now passed to Bushrod's nephew John Augustine Washington II and (after his death in 1832) to his wife, Jane Charlotte. To gain some small income, John Augustine and Jane Charlotte authorized Phil Smith to sell plants from the greenhouse (and advertised the fact in the *Alexandria Gazette*); elderly black people opened the gates at the porter's lodges and performed small services for visitors.[4]

Some of these people, like "Old Jenny," had once belonged to Bushrod Washington; others may have been among the last of the emancipated pensioners still on the estate. Americans and foreigners who made the pilgrimage to Mount Vernon from the 1830s on were more likely to interact with slaves than with Washingtons. By the 1840s, some northern visitors expressed horror at seeing "Slaves on the estate of Washington!" (as one exclaimed in her diary), interpreting the landscape through their own antipathy toward slavery. Others complained about black people's apparent expectation of gratuities for every minor courtesy.[5]

Unrecognized by most visitors, the second nineteenth-century African American community at Mount Vernon emerged in the 1840s and 1850s. John Augustine and Jane Charlotte's son John Augustine Washington III (known as Augustine) assumed management in 1841, hoping to restore the estate to agricultural profitability. Augustine transplanted people from his parents' Blakeley plantation in Jefferson County, Virginia, including young women and men who became field laborers. A number of them were members of the Parker family: in 1841, siblings Julia (b. 1823), Hannah (b. 1826), Edmund (1827–1898), and Betty (b. 1833), as well as their maternal grandmother, Betty, who became Mount Vernon's cook. Over the next two decades, at least five more Parker siblings and their mother, Milly, would also work at Mount Vernon. Hannah had eight children of her own by 1856, at least five of them with Warner May (1825–1888), whom Augustine purchased in 1846. Edmund would marry a woman named Susan (b. 1831), bought by Augustine in 1852; they would have six children before the Civil War. In addition to the extended Parker family, other families also grew: the dairymaid Sarah, inherited from Bushrod's estate, had five sons, one of whom, Joe Ford (b. 1832), had five children between 1853 and 1858. In all, Mount Vernon's enslaved population increased from fewer than twenty-five in 1842 to nearly eighty by 1858, while Augustine Washington more than tripled the cultivated acreage. African Americans performed agricultural and household labor not unlike that at other plantations; tasks varied by age, skill, and to some degree gender (though women as well as men worked in the fields). Mount Vernon in these years had two sets of slave quarters: one near the Mansion, visible to visitors; the other a mile north, abutting what Augustine called his "middle" fields, where much of the farm work occurred.

Enslaved men, women, and children were subject to Augustine Washington's economic strategies. He took his initial foray into the slave market-place in December 1842, purchasing a young man named Alfred (b. 1818) from his brother-in-law to be his valet or manservant. He sold Alfred barely two years later, citing an attempt to run off as the immediate cause. Over two decades he infrequently sold slaves, including two of the Parker siblings. More often he bought people, either individually or in family groups, including a woman named Matilda (b. 1819) with four children in 1852 and a butler named Nathan Johnson (1830–1885) with his wife and four children in 1856. (A seemingly humane gesture, purchasing family members together, sundered families and communities elsewhere: for example, Matilda had a husband and four other children whom Augustine did not buy.) From the early 1840s Augustine also leased out enslaved

NEGROES FOR HIRE.—A WOMAN who is a superior cook: one who is an excellent sempstress and washerwoman, and a fair cook; a GIRL of 16 or 18, who is accustomed to cooking and general housework. These servants are without incumbrance. Also. one or two children will be put out for a term of years, free of hire, to strictly responsible parties. Apply to   JOHN A. WASHINGTON,
dec 23—eotJanⱶ   Mount Vernou.

Notice by John Augustine Washington III in an 1856 issue of the Alexandria Gazette, *to hire out two of his enslaved women and a teenaged girl, as well as "one or two children" to be "put out … free of hire, to strictly responsible parties."*

people for several months or a year at a time, most often "hiring out" young women and girls who were not field-workers and who were superfluous in his household. At first he mostly hired out slaves to relatives and friends either near Mount Vernon or near Blakeley. Beginning in 1856, he advertised "negroes for hire" each December in the *Alexandria Gazette*, itemizing the people available for a year's rental.

One of those advertisements triggered a national fracas reminiscent of his great-uncle Bushrod's 1821 slave sale. By December 1858, the Mount Vernon Ladies' Association (MVLA) had contracted with Augustine to purchase the Washington Mansion and tomb along with two hundred acres, and the group had begun its nationwide campaign to raise the necessary $200,000. When the *New York Tribune* saw the advertisement entitled "negroes for hire—five women and girls and two boys," Horace Greeley editorialized that Mount Vernon had been "transmogrified into a regular slave shamble, where human beings are sold out to the highest bidder—the proprietor living on their wages."[6] To release the home of Washington from this stain, Greeley endorsed the MVLA's efforts. Other abolitionists countered that every dollar raised by the MVLA would line a slaveholder's pockets and encouraged benevolence to a higher cause. Indeed, the MVLA's money enabled Augustine Washington to buy Waveland, an 866-acre plantation in Fauquier County, for $35,000, and seven adult men and a thirteen-year-old boy for another $8,575.

Between 1858 and 1861, the Mount Vernon enslaved community was dislocated and dismembered again. As Augustine prepared to turn over the Mansion and surrounding grounds to the MVLA, he split his laboring force between Waveland and the thousand acres he retained at Mount Vernon. He left at Mount Vernon some twenty people, mostly farm laborers, while taking approximately forty others to Fauquier County, dividing families across sixty miles. After he was killed in September 1861 in the service of the Confederate States of America, his slaves endured the same ordeal as had Bushrod's: the division and sale of an owner's estate. At least eight people were sold in Richmond in late 1861 and early 1862; others may have been taken back to the Jefferson County plantation that belonged to Augustine's brother Richard Blackburn Washington, who became guardian to Augustine's seven children.

Still others returned to Mount Vernon—which now became their beacon of freedom. The people left on Augustine's land there found themselves beyond the executor's reach. With Alexandria having fallen to the Union, Augustine's Mount Vernon acreage became a sort of no-man's-land. Even before his death, some of the people at Waveland ran away to rejoin kin there. By July 1862 perhaps sixty men, women, and children lived on his abandoned land at Mount Vernon, cutting wood for money and reconstituting families. At least one of them, Andrew Ford (1843–1928, son of the dairymaid Sarah once owned by Bushrod Washington),

An unidentified Mount Vernon employee serves milk to visitors in the 1880s.

made his way to Michigan, where he enlisted in the First Michigan Colored Infantry. Several filed claims with the Freedmen's Bureau in the months after the war, asserting their rights to the fruits of their wartime labor.

After the war, people who had once belonged to Augustine Washington became employees of America's first historic house museum. Edmund Parker, who had come to Mount Vernon in 1841 as a fourteen-year-old field laborer, worked for the MVLA from the early 1870s until shortly before his death in 1898, becoming the guard at Washington's tomb and telling thousands of visitors about the site and its history. (He did not tell visitors that he had run away during the war to work for the Union Army.) Nathan Johnson, the butler Augustine purchased in 1856, returned in 1865 as "majordomo" of the Mansion, over which he presided until he died in 1885. His second wife, Sarah (1844–1920), was the daughter of Edmund Parker's sister Hannah, another of the teenaged field-workers transplanted from Blakeley in 1841. One of the teenaged girls Augustine hired out in the 1850s, Sarah worked for the MVLA from 1865 until 1892. She earned the confidence of the Ladies, for whom she cooked during their Council meetings and who consulted with her about matters ranging from curtains in the Mansion to the management of the male superintendent of the estate. She also operated a short-lived lunch business in the old kitchen and sold milk and guidebooks to visitors; she conveyed a sense of Old Virginia hospitality to visitors who craved the graciousness of the Washingtons' world. Ultimately, Sarah Johnson and several of her compatriots, also once enslaved at Mount Vernon, purchased land that had formerly belonged to George Washington's estate—completing the transition from slavery to freedom and self-determination even in the era of Jim Crow.

Thomas Bushrod took up the position of tomb guard after Edmund Parker's death in 1898.

Picturing George Washington, Mount Vernon, and Slavery

Maurie D. McInnis

The Old Mount Vernon, *painted by Eastman Johnson, 1857.*

In the first half of the nineteenth century, no person was more revered in the United States than George Washington, and no visage was more recognizable to Americans than his. As *pater patriae* he was universally admired and celebrated; his portrait, whether painting or print, graced the walls of American homes, both northern and southern. During his lifetime, he was most commonly represented in the guise of either general or president, sometimes accompanied by an enslaved attendant, much in the tradition of British aristocratic portraiture. The admiration for Washington only intensified after his death, so it is not surprising that opposing political sides used his likeness as a way to further their viewpoints. This is especially true for images concerning the question of slavery. In the heightened tensions of the 1850s, Washington was often depicted as a slave owner, and Mount Vernon as a place of enslavement. Competing visions emerge, however, and at the heart of that divide was whether slavery was a "positive good," as some advocates argued, or destructive for whites and blacks alike.[1]

Such imagery played an important role in shaping public opinion about Washington, and it continues to do so today. These depictions were not historically accurate. Rather, they were artistic creations intended to persuade their audiences. The most widely disseminated image of Washington as a slaveholder is *Washington as a Farmer, at Mount Vernon* by Junius Brutus Stearns (1810–1885). Although frequently used as an illustration of life at Mount Vernon in Washington's time, this 1851 paint-

Washington as a Farmer, at Mount Vernon, *painted by Junius Brutus Stearns, 1857*

ing tells us more about the politics of the 1850s than it does about its ostensible subject. The artist capitalized on the interest generated in 1849 by the fiftieth anniversary of Washington's death by painting a series depicting the former first president's life, including *The Marriage of Washington*; *Washington as a Farmer*; *Washington as a Soldier*; and *Washington on His Deathbed*. These images became well known and paid Stearns a handsome royalty through widely distributed lithographs published by M. Knoedler in 1853 and 1854.[2]

Images of Washington as a slave owner or farmer were not unknown, but it was rare and even radical to depict him so explicitly as a plantation slave master. In Stearns's picture, Washington's walking stick directs the viewer's attention to the central grouping of four slaves, one at work cutting wheat and three taking a break, drinking water from a pail with pewter tankards. The slaves in Washington's world, this image seems to suggest, are well cared for and content. They have no desire to run away.[3] Painted just after the passage of the Compromise of 1850, the divisive political deal fought over slavery and the admission of California as a free state, Stearns's *Washington as a Farmer* emphatically staked out a political position, telling viewers that Washington was a slave owner and that slavery was a benevolent and natural institution. Such an image contrasted starkly with Washington's own view, which he came to later in his life, that slavery ought to be abolished.

The artists Louis Rémy Mignot (1831–1870) and Thomas Rossiter (1843–1869) also depicted Washington as a benevolent slaveholder in *The Home of Washington after the War* (now known as *Washington and Lafayette at Mount Vernon, 1784*). Placing the retired general at the center, alongside his French comrade and ally, Mignot and Rossiter represented Washington within the domestic confines of the piazza in the company of his family and several slaves. The scene idealizes a period of national harmony, with the broad sweep of lawn and river beyond evoking the pastoral ideal.

Washington and Lafayette at Mount Vernon, 1784, *painted by Louis Rémy Mignot and Thomas Rossiter in 1859.*

In this imagined scene of two heroes just after the Revolutionary War, the artists emphasized Washington's status as a planter. In a written description, Rossiter underscored the representation of Washington as "the Hero [who] at once devoted himself to restoring his neglected estates, resuming the agricultural habits and pursuits of an opulent planter." This harmonious depiction of life at Mount Vernon belies the reality of enslavement on Washington's farms. Nowhere in this image is there a hint of the seventeen people from Mount Vernon who sought their freedom just a few years prior by escaping to the British frigate *Savage* in 1781 or those who resisted in numerous other ways.[4]

Both the Stearns and the Mignot/Rossiter images depict an idealized model plantation, rather than life at Mount Vernon for the enslaved residents. In 1793 Washington had written from Philadelphia of his desire for his slaves to work "from day-breaking until it is dusk in the evening," hoping that "every labourer (male or female) does as much in the 24 hours as their strength, without endangering their health, or constitution will allow of." Washington was a stern taskmaster, and from the mid-1780s to around 1800, two to three hundred people labored for him, producing a wide variety of crops (wheat, barley, corn, tobacco) and caring for the Washington family and the estate. The president's ambitious plans for remaking Mount Vernon and the associated quarter farms required an enormous effort from his enslaved labor force.[5]

Both paintings tie George Washington and Mount Vernon together, and in many images the plantation became almost synonymous with the man. The house, described as a "venerable structure, quite simple in its architecture, yet [it] impresses one deeply," was often seen as illustrative of Washington's noble republican simplicity.[6] Yet when Stearns visited in 1851 and Mignot in 1857, Mount Vernon was in a state of disrepair.

The east front of Mount Vernon Mansion, photographed in the 1850s. The standing figure may be John Augustine Washington III.

Willed by Washington to his nephew Bushrod Washington and still owned within that family, it had lost much of its luster; its crumbling character was described by one visitor in 1834 as "everything except the garden & interior of the house appears to be going to ruin."[7] Ignoring this reality, Stearns, Mignot, and Rossiter presented an idealized vision of Mount Vernon as Washington had wished it could be: a model plantation for a republic based on agricultural pursuits and enslaved labor. In their depiction, everyone benefited, both free and enslaved alike. Such images gave visual form and seeming verisimilitude to the argument that slavery was a "positive good."

Other artists derived different meanings from trips to Mount Vernon. Eastman Johnson, who visited in 1857 with his friend Mignot, chose not to represent George Washington at all. He emphasized the deteriorated condition of Mount Vernon, depicting the African American world of the estate. The Mount Vernon he saw was the 1850s plantation then owned by John Augustine Washington III, where seventy-six slaves lived and worked. The younger Washington was described in one New York newspaper as having "turned the home of the Father of his Country into a slaveholding pen."[8]

In *The Old Mount Vernon*, Johnson positions the viewer to the north side of the Mansion House (see page 100). This was a view not encountered by most visitors, who at that time arrived by steamship and proceeded to the house from the river. By shifting the focus to the side, Johnson completely transforms the viewer's experience. Rather than Washington's residence (the "big house"), it is the outbuilding and the connecting hyphen that fill the pictorial space. In the doorway sits an African American man; young children stand under the colonnade and in the yard. The white presence has been erased. Mount Vernon is no longer the embodiment of Washington's virtues; it is represented instead as a dilapidated "slaveholding pen."[9]

In Johnson's painting *Washington's Kitchen at Mount Vernon*, the viewer is led inside, where a young mother sits with her children. The darkened and gloomy scene shows a building in disrepair. Plaster has chipped off, revealing bricks and crumbling walls. The interior is largely unadorned; a few kitchen implements are strewn about. In some versions of the painting, a shadowy, indistinct image hangs over the fireplace. The latter detail is especially intriguing, given the long history in American paintings and prints of Washington's image shown hanging over a mantelpiece. Does his visage serve as a dark reminder of the founders' failed legacy in not dealing with slavery? Or was the image of the first president removed, thus revealing the crumbling institution of slavery without the guiding and benevolent hand of men such as Washington?

Johnson's images appear to be the painter's metaphoric commentary on the then-current state of the institution of slavery. Mount Vernon had for decades served as the symbolic embodiment of Washington and the virtues he represented. Now, the dilapidated buildings refer instead to the unhealthiness of slavery. As at many Virginia farms, the farms of Mount Vernon were exhausted by the 1850s. John Augustine Washington III found it difficult to earn a profit from the land. Hundreds of thousands of slaves had been sold from Virginia into the deep South, where they were put to work in the cotton and sugar fields.[10] Slavery in the Old Dominion was a different institution from what it had been during Washington's lifetime. Many antislavery activists argued that slavery destroyed both black and white lives, degrading and dehumanizing slaves and making whites self-indulgent, imperious, and indolent. Did Johnson see the decaying state of Mount Vernon as a comment on the impact of slavery on the South?

These differing images of George Washington's Mount Vernon, all painted during years of acrimonious debate about slavery, present differing visions of life at the estate. For modern audiences, they allow us to understand the continuing symbolic importance of the memory of George Washington for later generations. As the United States continues to grapple with the legacy of slavery, these images provide an opportunity for us as a nation to consider the meaning of enslavement at the home of the father of our country.

Washington's Kitchen at Mount Vernon, *painted by Eastman Johnson in 1864. Johnson's first version of this composition, painted in 1857, includes a framed picture over the fireplace. The scene actually depicts the interior of the north dependency, used as a (white) servants' hall in Washington's time.*

A Perspective on Mount Vernon Enslaved Ancestry

Rohulamin Quander, President, The Quander Historical Society, Inc.,
and Gloria Tancil Holmes, daughter of Gladys Quander Tancil

Rohulamin Quander seated before a portrait painted by his wife, Carmen Torruella-Quander.

The Quander family is pleased to be included in formulating the 2016 exhibition *Lives Bound Together: Slavery at George Washington's Mount Vernon.* The legacies of the many families who descended from the Mount Vernon enslaved community are both dynamic and diverse. As to the ancestors, there is no singular story related to those individuals that captures the depth and diversity of what they did and how their progeny turned out. As noted in cousin Lewis Lear Quander's poem "Legacy of Faith— A Tribute to My Mount Vernon Ancestors," which addresses the ancestral contributions: "Some were kitchen hands; Some worked with wood and some with cans; Some dug ditches; some fixed fences, down where the dismal swamp commences. With straw and mud they put together bricks that have withstood the weather; and houses they built from the ground through all these years are still around."

Time and effort have shown their descendants to be capable of heretofore undreamed-of accomplishments. From medical doctors to lawyers and judges, plus pastors and bishops, to school teachers and principals, and also three U.S. Army generals, two of whom are West Point graduates, Quander family members are experiencing all of this. This is the legacy of Suckey Bay of River Farm, her husband, Carter, a non-Washington slave, and their daughters Rose and Nancy Carter, and the latter's husband, Charles Quander, a free black man.

Historically, the many legacies that Mount Vernon helped to create were a two-edged sword. On one edge was the continuation of the evil institution thought to be permanently dedicated to the care of the Washington family. On the converse side, being in the presence of General Washington and his family created a yearning, an internal drive for something significantly more. We were not focused solely upon how we, as Washington's "servants," could learn to be better servants as much as we yearned to become men and women of service, which we have.

Our sentiment is that history must hold Washington accountable for the deficiencies of his action, as someone who enslaved human beings. History has well noted his shortcoming in this respect. But as Quanders, we cannot view him in solely one dimension. A man of his time, located in Virginia and presiding over the operation of one of the greatest estates in United States history, he could not have managed his affairs without forced labor. The larger picture likewise tells the greater story. Not only is it a story of chains and shackles, but it is also a story of triumph over tragedy, even if it took well more than a century for the magnitude of the fuller story to emerge.

Only when the Slave Memorial was built and dedicated in 1983 was there acknowledgment that slaves lived, worked, and contributed to the home of George Washington. Before then, Mount Vernon's slaves were euphemistically referred to as "servants." In 1995–1996, Gladys Quander Tancil, the first African American historical interpreter employed at Mount Vernon, conducted the first slave life tours. It was her ultimate desire to interpret the lives of Mount Vernon slaves with all honesty and dignity while conducting her tours. She set a tone and standard of expanded respect for the contributions of the enslaved who served the Washington family. On June 21, 1996, Sekila Holmes Argrett, Gladys Tancil's granddaughter, carried the Olympic torch at Mount Vernon in memory of the many unsung enslaved.

Some years ago, during one of the annual Quander family reunions, an interviewer asked, "How do the Quanders feel today about the fact that George Washington permanently enslaved several of your ancestors, denying them even the rudiments of education?" The response was largely universal. Family, noting that Washington was a man of his time, still held him accountable for his action of upholding the evils of human bondage. Further, while recognizing his greatness as the father of our country, many acknowledged his major step towards moving away from permanent enslavement by setting an example and freeing those who involuntarily served him, although not until his own death.

Gloria Tancil Holmes.

Gladys Quander Tancil leading tour group along Mount Vernon's north lane.

In 2010 the 85th Quander family reunion was held at the Mount Vernon estate, garnering national media attention. Activities included laying a memorial wreath at the slave burial site and a private viewing of the Quander genealogy tree, which once hung in the Smithsonian Institution's Museum of American History in Washington, D.C. Quanders from all over the county attended the events. Mount Vernon has included Quander family members in a variety of activities highlighting Mount Vernon slave life, such as wreath laying, the formal opening of a slave cabin, and the rededication of a remodeled slave quarter.

The legacy of our forebears, both living and deceased, challenges Quanders to live up to expectations. The legacy requires a focus, a commitment to excellence, and a record of sustained achievement. Quander family members are still on this mission. The beacon burns brightly; the path to success remains well lighted. But we must, by our own individual and collective examples, inspire others to join us on the way. For only by conducting ourselves in this manner can we come to fully appreciate what it means "To Be a Quander."

Sekila Holmes Argrett carries the Olympic torch at Mount Vernon in 1996.

The Mount Vernon Legacy

ZSun-nee Matema

I've always wondered what it was about my childhood experience at Mount Vernon that made me feel at home. I've since come to believe there is not only a genetic connection to our ancestors but a psychic one as well. I didn't learn about my Caroline until I became an adult. My father's side of the family held all of the secrets about her and subsequent generations. However, like many African American families, they kept what they knew secret, especially from the children. If we were lucky, we found bits and pieces of our ancestors in journals, diaries, or from eavesdropping. Uncovering the life of an enslaved ancestor was not considered a thing of pride as little as twenty years ago.

Even so, it appears many on my father's side of the family knew very little about their enslaved ancestors at Mount Vernon. This brings to mind the absolute necessity of researching family history. What I did learn about my father's side of the family came from my aunt Juanita. When I asked her about the family, she indicated that it was complicated, the kind of thing one would read about in a novel. She also said that we were connected to the top families of Virginia. That was all she said, and I was too young at the time to ask the right questions.

It was shocking for me to learn what slavery really meant. The many layers of slavery slice through the human mind. They lay bare many raw emotions of discrimination and shame and loss of identity. I knew only what I'd been taught in school. That wasn't very much, and what there was certainly did not make me feel proud.

I remember it as if it were yesterday. I walked into the Alexandria Black History Resource Center in Alexandria, Virginia, to conduct business for Arena Stage. I was there on a mission. I wanted to encourage the African American community in Alexandria to become Arena subscribers. Little did I know the mission was not what I brought with me but what was waiting for me.

I was met at the door by the curator of the Resource Center, Audrey Davis. She pointed out the small library and told me that the Resource Center grew out of it. I walked in and noticed a letter on the wall from someone I recognized as an ancestor, requesting money from African

ZSun-nee Matema at Mount Vernon's slave cemetery.

American businessmen to develop the library. As I waited to make my pitch for an onsite program bringing Arena actors to the Center, I noticed a portrait over the entrance to the small library. Noting the name, I asked if the Robert Henry Robinson pictured, and the man for whom the library was named, was in any way connected to Magnus Lewis Robinson, my great-grandfather. To my amazement, Audrey said that he was Magnus Robinson's father. Then she asked if I knew who Robert Robinson's parents were. I said no. Then she asked if I knew who his grandparents were. I thought to myself, *I didn't know who he was until just a few minutes ago,* so I said that I knew nothing about his ancestry. She then said, "Well, sit down." She went downstairs to storage and brought up several thick files. She plopped them on the table and said, "Enjoy!"

That day, very little business was conducted for Arena Stage. The first thing I saw in one of the files was a library commemoration program featuring the renovation events. It contained a short biography of my great-great-grandfather. Then I saw what changed my life forever: "Robert Henry Robinson was the grandson of Caroline Branham, a personal maid to Martha Washington." My heart stopped. Could this be true? Then I remembered that early school trip where, as a child, I skipped back and forth at the entrance to Mount Vernon. I only remember saying to myself, "This is home. This is home." And to this day, Mount Vernon is what lives in my heart.

An entire world then opened to me. One rich with the fabric of time and full with the passion of people who lived, worked, and supported the efforts at Mount Vernon. I met Mary Thompson, historian at Mount Vernon. What a wonderful day that was for me. Mary began sending me a stream of white paper through my fax machine; the pages were filled with facts and glimpses of life in another time. It was a world I had only glimpsed in historical novels.

It was then that I was introduced to my Caroline and my family's history at Mount Vernon. Learning about succeeding generations became a priority in my life. I turned back time to discover the duties, accomplishments, and lifestyles of my ancestors. For eight years I searched through public libraries, courthouse records, and newspaper clippings. I spoke with everyone who could shed light on my Caroline's life at Mount Vernon. Many exciting opportunities opened for me to learn about not only her life but the lives of General and Mrs. Washington. Just as important was to explore the available resources of the wonderful Mount Vernon staff.

Through reenactments, panels, videos, and presentations I began to feel a part of the history created by my ancestor Caroline Branham. What I have learned in the meantime has only enlarged her presence and the meaning of life as an enslaved person. Personal accounts of visitors to Mount Vernon brought to the forefront her sense of humor and her ability to tell a good story. I, too, am a storyteller.

The day-to-day tasks my Caroline was responsible for were relegated to maintaining the integrity of the house. The daily chores of cleaning, polishing, making beds, sewing, and attending to the needs of numerous houseguests were consuming. In other words, when the enslaved people who worked the fields were given Sundays off, house servants were ever on duty. It gives new meaning to the term house slaves, who, I assumed before knowing, had more time to themselves.

I learned that Robert Henry Robinson, Caroline's grandson, was released early. This detail mystified me until I learned that the noted Washington biographer Jared Sparks had asked Caroline to give an accounting of Washington's last hours. It seems she was in the room when he died. Her reward for the interview was the release of her grandson, my great-great-grandfather. This led to an interest in the last hours of General Washington's life. I learned that Caroline was sent to bring the doctor to Mount Vernon on the morning of Washington's death. She acted as doorkeeper, allowing people deemed appropriate into the room. As the day drew into night, Caroline was in and out of the room where the general lay dying and would certainly have had knowledge about his condition.

Believed to have been used in the Washingtons' bedchamber, this Windsor chair was acquired by the Mount Vernon Ladies' Association in 1892 from Lucy Harrison, a free African American woman and daughter of enslaved Mount Vernon housemaid Caroline Branham, who was in the bedchamber when George Washington died.

When attempting to tell my grandchildren about slavery, I first let them know that people are not born slaves. Slaves are created and are therefore enslaved. At age six, my granddaughter Harmony joined me for the opening of the slave quarters at Mount Vernon. She was to give a short speech on our Caroline. On the way there, she asked poignantly, "Why slavery, Lesee?" I didn't know how to answer that question. I couldn't find one answer that I thought would satisfy her young mind. I struggled. I wanted her to know the fullness of Caroline's life, but not at the expense of forgetting that slavery meant the loss of freedom and the increase of limitation which enslaved people most certainly felt.

I tried to explain to her that many enslaved people were captured in Africa and sold here in America. Some were Native Americans who came from various counties of Virginia and were "bounded out" to wealthy families for instruction in household duties. In some way, I wanted my granddaughter to know that people were born free, but because captors, enslavers, or communities had made arrangements that devalued them, they became tethered to other people who owned them and that it was not always for their good.

What I really want, now that I have learned so much more, is for my grandchildren and great-grandchildren to know that everything we are is a culmination of who our ancestors were. That genetic and psychic connection will forever link us to them. The relationships they embellished, enjoyed, and extricated themselves from are all part of the journey. Caroline was fortunate in some ways. Her life at Mount Vernon, from what I can discern, was not a life characterized by brutal hardship. Yet she was enslaved and therefore unable to live her life as she would wish or dream. Within the confines of slavery, she found a way of managing her life so that she loved, married, and gave birth to generations of children who, because of her and her place at Mount Vernon, were respected.

Caroline's daughter Lucy gave birth to Robert Henry Robinson. After being emancipated, he was apprenticed to the Jamieson Bakery in Old Town Alexandria. It is said that Queen Victoria insisted on getting her crackers and baked goods from this establishment. I've often smiled to myself to think that she may well have enjoyed a box of crackers prepared by my great-great-grandfather. Robert H. Robinson went on to become the first ordained minister from Robert's Memorial United Methodist Chapel in Alexandria and pastored nineteen United Methodist churches. He was the youngest grandmaster in the Washington, D.C./Alexandria, Virginia, Masonic order.

His son Magnus Lewis Robinson became a writer, business owner, newspaper publisher, and editor. Most notably he published the *National Leader*, a Republican newspaper. He held several offices among the Republican Party in Harrisonburg, Virginia, as well as in Alexandria and created the John Hay School, later named the William McKinley School.

Magnus's daughter, my grandmother Mary Virginia Robinson, was a homemaker, carrying on the skills and creative talents of Caroline. She raised three children; her youngest, Emmett Robinson Miller, was my father, a culinary artist. He joined his brother Joseph Miller, co-owner of a restaurant in northwest Washington, D.C. In his later years, he worked for the Irish Embassy in Washington, D.C.

General Washington, politician, first president of the United States, farmer and landowner . . . owned people. That is still a fact. The legacy of Mount Vernon is an ongoing connection that continues to instill a special sense of pride in the building and maintaining of Mount Vernon to the descendants of the enslaved. Without them, General Washington would not have been able to leave his farm estates and do the work that made a country we can call our own. George Washington made "The People," as he called his enslaved people, great by association. My ancestors' skills and determination to benefit from that association is what made them key stockholders in the American Dream.

As an educator, historic preservationist, writer, cultural artist, and transformational trainer, I know that everything I am has been passed down, mind to mind, experience to experience, from my Caroline and eventually to me. Mount Vernon will always shine a light on me. It will always be home.

Appendix

Selected Timeline of George Washington and Slavery at Mount Vernon

This chronology highlights key events in the lives of people enslaved at Mount Vernon as well as George Washington's public and private actions relating to slavery. Both are set in context with landmark moments in the history of the United States.

Red = enslaved people at Mount Vernon
Green = landmark historical events
Brown = Washington's private actions
Black = **Washington's public actions**

1619 Enslaved Africans first brought to Virginia and sold at Jamestown.

1705 The Virginia legislature enacts a slave code, establishing systematic rules for relationships between slaves and citizens.

1743 George Washington, age 11, is bequeathed slaves upon the death of his father, Augustine Washington.

1750 Washington, age 18, gains legal control of 11 people from his father's estate: Fortune, George, Long Joe, Winna, Bellindar, Jenny, Adam, Nat, London, Milly, and Frank.

1754 Washington inherits 6 slaves from his half-brother, Lawrence Washington: Peter, Jenny, Tom (Jenny's son), Phebe, Tom, and Lucy. He leases another 18 slaves from Lawrence's estate.
Washington leases Mount Vernon from the estate of his half-brother, Lawrence.

1755 **Washington participates in the disastrous Braddock expedition to the Ohio Valley.**

1757 Virginia planter Daniel Parke Custis dies, leaving no will. His widow, Martha Dandridge Custis, receives a life-interest in one-third of his estate, which includes almost 300 enslaved people spread across plantations in six counties.

1758 Washington completes his first expansion of the Mount Vernon Mansion.

1759 George Washington and Martha Dandridge Custis marry and settle at Mount Vernon. Martha probably brings at least 12 enslaved

One of Washington's agricultural experiments required enslaved field workers to plant wheat in clumps, as re-created at Mount Vernon's Pioneer Farm.

artisans and domestic workers with her, including Doll, a cook, and Sally, Martha's maid. George Washington gains legal control (but not ownership) of the whole of the Custis estate, including the people, property, income, and goods inherited by Martha's young children. Washington purchases at least 12 additional slaves.

1761   Peros, Jack, Neptune, and Cupid (all native Africans) run away from Dogue Run Farm. Peros, Jack, and Cupid are back in 1762, but Neptune appears to have evaded recapture until 1765.

1762   George Washington inherits 5 slaves from Lawrence Washington's widow, Ann Fairfax Washington Lee: Kate, George, Maria, and Kate's two children (unnamed) return to Mount Vernon after an absence of 8 years.

1763   The French and Indian War ends.
        Washington begins reducing tobacco production, replacing it with wheat.

1765   British Parliament passes the Stamp Act. The Virginia legislature responds with Resolves protesting "taxation without representation."
        Washington decides to cease tobacco production and make wheat his primary cash crop; he also expands hemp and flax growing to support large-scale textile production. He calls the Stamp Act "a direful attack upon [the colonists'] Liberties."

1766   Washington appoints the first of several enslaved overseers. Tom, a foreman at River Farm, attempts to run away and is captured. Washington sells him in the West Indies.

1768   Washington purchases William (Billy) Lee, who becomes Washington's valet, and his brother Frank Lee, who becomes Mount Vernon's butler.

1774   Washington begins adding wings onto the two ends of the Mansion.

1775   The 2nd Continental Congress names Washington commander in chief of the Continental Army.
        In October, the Council of War, headed by Washington, prohibits "Negroes" from enlisting in the army. This prohibition is reversed in December, permitting free blacks to enlist if approved by Congress.
        In November, Virginia's royal governor, Lord Dunmore, issues proclamation offering freedom to enslaved men who serve with the British military.

1776   Washington corresponds with Phillis Wheatley, an enslaved woman, praising a poem she had written in his honor.
        The 2nd Continental Congress adopts the Declaration of Independence, proclaiming: "We hold these truths to be self-evident, that all men are created equal, that they are endowed by their Creator with

certain unalienable Rights, that among these are Life, Liberty and the pursuit of Happiness."

Washington leads a daring nighttime crossing of the Delaware River and defeats the British at Trenton.

1777 Alexander Hamilton, John Laurens and the Marquis de Lafayette join Washington's military staff, introducing antislavery ideas.

1778 Washington writes privately that "I wish to get quit of Negroes"—the earliest documented expression of a desire to no longer own slaves.

1780 Pennsylvania passes the Act for the Gradual Abolition of Slavery, prohibiting importation of new slaves into the state and freeing children born into slavery once they reach adulthood. The act permits non-resident slaveholders to keep their slaves in Pennsylvania for no more than six months, at which point slaves can claim their freedom.

1781 17 Mount Vernon slaves (Peter, Lewis, Frank, Frederick, Gunner, Harry, Tom, Sambo, Thomas, Peter, Stephen, James, Watty, Daniel, Lucy, Esther, and Deborah) flee aboard the British ship *Savage*, on the Potomac River. 7 of them (Frederick, Frank, Gunner, Sambo, Thomas, Lucy, and Esther) are eventually returned to Mount Vernon, while 3 (Daniel, Deborah, and Harry) escape from New York with the British. The fate of the others remains unknown.

British General Lord Cornwallis surrenders his army at Yorktown, the last major battle of the Revolutionary War.

En route to and from Yorktown, Washington spends a few days at Mount Vernon—his only visits during the Revolutionary War.

1782 The state of Virginia passes legislation permitting slaveowners to free slaves without a special act of the general assembly.

1783 The Treaty of Paris formally ends the American Revolution.

Washington resigns his military commission and returns to Mount Vernon.

Washington privately expresses admiration for the Marquis de Lafayette's plan for the abolition of slavery.

1785 Washington refuses to sign an antislavery petition presented by Methodist abolitionists.

He begins creating a picturesque landscape at Mount Vernon, echoing English country estates.

1786 Washington installs bookcases in his study and begins finishing the New Room of the Mansion. He privately states his support for the gradual abolition of slavery via legislative action.

In his diary, he lists all of the enslaved people belonging to himself and to the Custis estate: a total of 216 people, including 90 under the age of 14.

1787   Washington presides over the Constitutional Convention, at which the status of enslaved people in the United States is hotly debated. Delegates agree to the Three-Fifths Compromise, which counts one enslaved person as equal to 3/5 of one free person for the apportionment of each state's congressional representatives as allocated by population for the House of Representatives.

1788   French abolitionist Jacques-Pierre Brissot de Warville likely presents Washington with Thomas Clarkson's *Essay on the Impolicy of the African Slave Trade*, one of six antislavery pamphlets that Washington binds together in a volume entitled, "Tracts on Slavery."

1789   Washington is elected the first president of the United States.
       The Washingtons take several enslaved servants to the first national capital, in New York.

1790   The president's household, including Oney Judge, Moll, Christopher Sheels, Austin, Giles, Paris, Hercules, and Richmond, moves to the second national capital, in Philadelphia.
       Washington privately writes that Quaker-led antislavery petitions to Congress are, "not only an ill-judged piece of business, but [they] occasioned a great waste of time."

1791   The Bill of Rights is ratified.
       Washington instructs his secretary to send slaves from the president's household back to Mount Vernon, thus evading the Pennsylvania law that would have allowed them to claim freedom after six-months residence in the state. Several of those affected belong to the Custis estate.
       Washington sends Jack, an enslaved wagoner, to the West Indies "to be disposed of."
       Giles, a postilion, accompanies Washington on his tour of the southern states.

1793   Washington condones his farm manager's having whipped the enslaved housemaid, Charlotte, for being "very impudent." He also directs the farm manager to threaten another slave with sale in the West Indies, "if a stop is not put to his rogueries, & other villainies."
       Enslaved overseer Davy Gray advocates for more rations for enslaved people, and Washington increases the rations.
       As president, Washington signs the Fugitive Slave Act into law, granting slaveholders the right to pursue runaway slaves even if they have escaped to free states or territories.
       Eli Whitney invents the cotton gin.

1794   Washington signs the Slave Trade Act into law, prohibiting American ships from engaging in the slave trade. Foreign ships continue to bring slaves to the United States, but cannot export them.

Enslaved overseer Will asks Washington if his wife, Kate, a field-worker, can serve as the midwife for the enslaved community.

1796 Oney Judge, Martha Washington's personal maid, escapes from the president's house in Philadelphia, eventually settling in New Hampshire.

Washington advertises to rent his outlying four farms, aiming to use the proceeds to free his slaves.

1797 Hercules, the Washingtons' enslaved cook, escapes from Mount Vernon, where he had been temporarily reassigned as a laborer.

Washington completes his second term as president and retires to Mount Vernon.

Christopher Sheels, Washington's valet, is sent with money to Lebanon, Pennsylvania, to receive treatment after it was feared he had contracted rabies.

1799 Washington composes a list recording each enslaved person on the estate, which farm he or she lives on, and whether owned by Washington or the Custis estate. In July, he writes a new will, directing that William Lee be freed immediately upon Washington's own death, and that the remainder of his slaves be freed upon Martha's death.

In August, Washington writes privately about the challenges in divesting himself of slaves: "To sell the overplus I cannot, because I am principled against this kind of traffic in the human species. To hire them out, is almost as bad, because they could not be disposed of in families to any advantage, and to disperse the families I have an aversion. What then is to be done? Something must, or I shall be ruined…"

In December, Washington dies of a throat infection.

1801 Martha Washington frees the slaves that belonged to her husband.

1802 Martha Washington dies, ending her life-rights to the Custis estate. The Custis slaves are dispersed to her heirs.

1808 Congress prohibits U.S. participation in the international slave trade.

1831 Nat Turner leads slave revolt in Virginia.

1833 Great Britain emancipates slaves throughout the British empire.

1852 Harriet Beecher Stowe's *Uncle Tom's Cabin* is published.

1860 The Mount Vernon Ladies' Association purchases Mount Vernon from John Augustine Washington III.

1861 Confederate States secede from the Union and war begins.

1865 War ends and the 13th Amendment to the Constitution abolishes slavery in the United States.

Abbreviations and Frequently Cited Sources

The voluminous primary sources relating to George and Martha Washington and Mount Vernon have long been dispersed among many repositories, published in numerous formats, and cited inconsistently by earlier authors. To minimize confusion and aid general readers interested in consulting the relevant documents, we have endeavored to apply standard terminology and to cite online versions whenever they are available.

Cash Memoranda, 1794–97	George Washington, Cash Memoranda, Sept. 29, 1794–Aug. 31, 1797 [photostats], vol. 29-A, Washington Library, from original manuscripts at John Carter Brown Library, Providence, RI
Cash Memoranda, 1797–99	George Washington, Cash Memoranda, Sept. 1, 1797–Dec. 3, 1799 [photostats], vol. 31-A, Washington Library, from original manuscripts at John Carter Brown Library, Providence, RI
"Drafts of Negros," 1802	"List of the different Drafts of Negros" [ca. 1802], in scrapbook, box 34, Peter Family Archives, Washington Library
Fairfax County Register of Free Blacks	Donald Sweig, ed., *"Registrations of Free Negroes Commencing September Court 1822, Book No. 2" and "Register of Free Blacks 1835 in Book 3": Being the Full Text of the Two Extant Volumes, 1822–1861, of Registrations of Free Blacks Now in the County Courthouse, Fairfax, Virginia* (Fairfax, VA: History Section, Office of Comprehensive Planning, Fairfax County, 1977)
GW	George Washington
GWD	*The Diaries of George Washington*, ed. Donald Jackson and Dorothy Twohig, 6 vols. (Charlottesville: Univ. Press of Virginia, 1976–79)
Ledger Book 1	Ledger Book 1, 1750–72, George Washington Papers, 1741–99, Series 5: Financial Papers, 1750–96, Library of Congress, Washington, DC; memory.loc.gov/ammem/gwhtml/gwseries5.html. Also known as Ledger A
Ledger Book 2	Ledger Book 2, 1772–93, George Washington Papers, 1741–99, Series 5: Financial Papers, 1750–96, Library of Congress, Washington, DC; memory.loc.gov/ammem/gwhtml/gwseries5.html. Also known as Ledger B

LOC	Library of Congress, Washington, DC
MNHP	Morristown National Historical Park, Morristown, NJ
MV	Mount Vernon
MVLA	The Mount Vernon Ladies' Assiciation of the Union
MW	Martha Washington
PGWDE	*The Papers of George Washington, Digital Edition*, ed. Theodore J. Crackel, Edward G. Lengel, et al. (Charlottesville: Univ. of Virginia Press, Rotunda, 2008)
PGW, Colonial Series	*The Papers of George Washington, Colonial Series*, ed. W.W. Abbot et al., 6 vols. (Charlottesville: Univ. Press of Virginia, 1992–97)
Washington Library	Fred W. Smith National Library for the Study of George Washington, Mount Vernon, VA
"Washington's Slave List," 1799	George Washington, "Negros Belonging to George Washington in his own right and by Marriage" [June 1799]
WGW	*The Writings of George Washington, from the Original Manuscript Sources, 1745–1799*, ed. John C. Fitzpatrick, 39 vols. (Washington, DC: U.S. Government Printing Office, 1931–44)
WMQ	*William and Mary Quarterly*

Notes

BIOGRAPHIES

Whenever possible, the biographical narratives use the term "enslaved person" to emphasize the humanity of each individual: they were people first and not solely defined by their lack of freedom. The words "slave" or "slaves" are used when they appear in historical quotations; to refer to legal, social, or economic statuses; or when using "enslaved" would be unclear or linguistically awkward. Spelling, capitalization, and punctuation in quotations have been retained as written in the original sources.

1. A note on last names: only a small number of enslaved people at Mount Vernon had surnames documented in George Washington's records. The origin of these names is often unclear. They may have come from a previous master, a father who was free, or a family tradition. In some cases individuals' last names do not appear until the nineteenth century, though it is unknown whether the surnames were chosen in that period or had been passed down privately within enslaved families but not documented by eighteenth-century recordkeepers. For this reason, we have chosen to use last names whenever possible for the people featured in this volume, even when those names do not appear in Washington's documentation. We use first names when no surname is known or for clarity, especially to distinguish among members of the same family.

2. GW, Cash Accounts, May 3, 1768, *PGWDE*, n2. If not specifically cited, biographical and genealogical information about enslaved people has been drawn from Washington's 1786 and 1799 slave lists: GW, Diary, Feb. 18, 1786, and "Washington's Slave List," 1799, *PGWDE*; the MV slavery database, which compiles references to the estate's enslaved people; and the files of Mary V. Thompson, Mount Vernon's research historian. On the database, see Molly Kerr's essay, "The Tiniest of Details," in this volume.

3. For reference to Frank as "mulatto," see GW to William Pearce, October 27, 1793, *PGWDE*. The identities of Frank and William Lee's parents are unknown.

4. Philip D. Morgan and Michael L. Nicholls, "Slave Flight: Mount Vernon, Virginia, and the Wider Atlantic World," in *George Washington's South*, ed. Tamara Harvey and Greg O'Brien (Gainesville: Univ. Press of Florida, 2004), 212.

5. MW to Frances (Fanny) Bassett Washington, Nov. 11, 1794, in Joseph E. Fields, *"Worthy Partner": The Papers of Martha Washington* (Westport, CT: Greenwood Press, 1994), 279–80.

6. An Inventory and Appraisement of the estate of Genl. George Washington Deceased, ca. 1799, probated 1810; transcription, Gunston Hall Plantation Probate Inventory Data Base; accessed March 7, 2016, gunstonhall.org/library/probate/WSHGTN99.PDF.

7. Edward C. Carter II and Angeline Polites, eds., *The Virginia Journals of Benjamin Henry Latrobe, 1795–1798* (New Haven, CT: Yale Univ. Press for the Maryland Historical Society, 1977), vol. 1, plate 20, fig. 27.

8. GW to William Pearce, Oct. 27, 1793, *PGWDE*.

9. MW to Fanny Bassett Washington, Aug. 4, 1793, in Fields, *"Worthy Partner,"* 250–51.

10. "Drafts of Negros," 1802.

11. *Alexandria Gazette*, July 30, 1821.

12. GW, Memorandum, "List of Artisans and Household Slaves in the Estate" [ca. 1759], Settlement of the Daniel Parke Custis Estate, Schedule III-C, *PGWDE*.

13. In Washington's 1786 list of enslaved workers, he describes Doll as "almost past service"; Hercules and Nathan are listed as the estate's cooks; GW, Diary, Feb. 18, 1786, *PGWDE*.

14. GW to Anthony Whitting (Whiting), May 12, 1793, *PGWDE*; MW to Fanny Bassett Washington, May 24, 1795, in Fields, "*Worthy Partner*," 287–88.

15. Doll was a common name among enslaved women, making it difficult to track her fate.

16. "Drafts of Negros," 1802.

17. GW to William Pearce, June 5, 1796, *WGW*, 35:79.

18. Mary G. Powell, *The History of Old Alexandria, Virginia, From July 13, 1749, to May 24, 1861* (Richmond, VA: William Byrd Press, 1928), 76–78.

19. Tobias Lear, "The last illness and Death of General Washington, Journal Account," Dec. 15, 1799, *PGWDE*.

20. Credit entries, Sept. 24, 1792 and July 2, 1793, Ledger Book 2, folios 345R, 368R (images 689, 735); entry for Aug. 18, 1797, Cash Memoranda, 1794–97, p. 30a; entry for June 3, 1799, Cash Memoranda, 1797–99, p. 96.

21. GW to David Stuart, Jan. 22, 1788, *PGWDE*.

22. "Drafts of Negros," 1802. One of Caroline's descendants, Zsun-nee Matema, reflects on her family's history in an essay, "The Mount Vernon Legacy," in this volume.

23. For an overview of these changes, see Philip Morgan's essay, "George Washington and Slavery," in this volume.

24. The Slave Trade Act of 1794 banned ships originating in American ports from participating in the trafficking of human cargo. This legislation was part of a series of laws culminating in 1808, when the United States outlawed the importation of enslaved Africans.

25. GW, Cash Accounts, May 3, 1768, *PGWDE*, n2. Though the name "Billy Lee" appears frequently in popular histories and is well known, George Washington only referred to his valet by that diminutive until about 1771. After that date, Washington almost exclusively called him "Will" or "William." Compare GW, Memorandum, List of Tithables, ca. June 14, 1771, *PGWDE*, which lists "Billy" as a house servant, with GW, Memorandum, List of Tithables, ca. June 10, 1772, *PGWDE* (and subsequent lists), which record "Will." There is also evidence that William Lee himself preferred that name. In his will, Washington noted, "And to my Mulatto man William (calling himself William Lee) I give immediate freedom"; GW, Last Will and Testament, July 9, 1799, *PGWDE*.

26. George Washington Parke Custis and Mary Custis Lee, *Recollections and Private Memoirs of Washington* (Philadelphia: J. W. Bradley, 1861), 224, 387.

27. Custis and Lee, *Recollections*, 450–51.

28. GW to Clement Biddle, July 28, 1784, *PGWDE*.

29. GW, Diary, Apr. 22, 1785; Mar. 1, 1788, *PGWDE*.

30. Tobias Lear to Clement Biddle, May 3, 1789, *PGWDE*.

31. In 1799 Washington identified "Will" as the shoemaker and described him as "lame"; "Washington's Slave List," 1799, *PGWDE*.

32. GW, Last Will and Testament, July 9, 1799, *PGWDE*.

33. Eugene E. Prussing, *The Estate of George Washington, Deceased* (Boston, MA: Little, Brown, 1927), 159.

34. "Visit to Mount Vernon," *Western Literary Messenger* 6, no. 13 (May 2, 1846): 201.

35. Many questions surround the creation and subject of this portrait. Stuart scholars question the attribution to the artist, and the origin of the painting's connection to Hercules and George Washington is not well documented. Further research may reveal more information about the portrait's history.

36. GW, Diary, Feb. 18, 1786, *PGWDE*.

37. MV Store Book, Sept. 9, 1787, Washington Library.

38. GW to Tobias Lear, Sept. 17, 1790, *PGWDE*.

39. Custis and Lee, *Recollections*, 422–24.

40. Tobias Lear to GW, June 5, 1791, *PGWDE*.

41. GW to William Pearce, Nov. 14, 1796, *WGW*, 35:278.

42. James Anderson to GW, Weekly Report, Feb. 25, 1797, in MV Farm Accounts [photostats], Jan. 7, 1797–Sept. 10, 1797, vol. 10-F, p. 39, Washington Library, from original manuscript at MNHP.

43. "1797. 'They Hoped They Would No Longer Be Slaves in Ten Years': Louis-Philippe," in *Experiencing Mount Vernon: Eyewitness Accounts, 1784–1865*, ed. Jean B. Lee (Charlottesville: Univ. of Virginia Press, 2006), 68.

44. "Drafts of Negros," 1802.

45. Benjamin Chase, letter to the editor, *The Liberator*, Jan. 1, 1847, quoted as "Mrs [?] Staines," in *Slave Testimony: Two Centuries of Letters, Speeches, Interviews, and Autobiographies*, ed. John W. Blassingame (Baton Rouge: Louisiana State Univ. Press, 1977), 248–50.

46. Lund Washington to GW, Oct. 15 and 22, 1775, *PGWDE*; Lund Washington, Account Book [microform], 1772–86, Washington Library. On naming practices, see n. 1 above.

47. Chase, letter to the editor, 1847; Frederick Kitt, "Advertisement," *Philadelphia Gazette and Universal Daily Advertiser*, May 24, 1796.

48. GW to Oliver Wolcott, Sept. 1, 1796, *WGW*, 35:201–2.

49. GW to Tobias Lear, Apr. 12, 1791, *PGWDE*.

50. See "References to People from the Presidential Household Account Books," *The President's House in Philadelphia*, accessed March 7, 2016, ushistory.org/presidentshouse/history/references.htm.

51. T. H. Adams, "Washington's Runaway Slave, and How Portsmouth Freed Her," *Granite Freeman*, May 22, 1845, reprinted in *Frank W. Miller's Portsmouth New Hampshire Weekly*, June 2, 1877.

52. Kitt, "Advertisement," 1796.

53. Kitt, "Advertisement," 1796; Adams, "Washington's Runaway Slave."

54. Adams, "Washington's Runaway Slave."

55. GW to Oliver Wolcott, Sept. 1, 1796, *WGW*, 35:201–2.

56. Joseph Whipple to Oliver Wolcott, Oct. 4, 1796, quoted in Fritz Hirschfeld, *George Washington and Slavery: A Documentary Portrayal* (Columbia: Univ. of Missouri Press, 1997), 114–15.

57. GW to Joseph Whipple, Nov. 28, 1796, quoted in Hirschfeld, *George Washington and Slavery,* 115–16.

58. GW to Joseph Whipple, Nov. 28, 1796, quoted in Hirschfeld, *George Washington and Slavery,* 115–16.

59. GW to Burwell Bassett Jr., Aug. 11, 1799, *PGWDE.*

60. Chase, letter to the editor, 1847.

61. Chase, letter to the editor, 1847.

62. "Drafts of Negros," 1802.

63. Adams, "Washington's Runaway Slave."

64. Anthony Whitting to GW, Jan. 22, 1792, *PGWDE.*

65. See Eleanor Breen's essay, "The Archaeology of Enslavement," in this volume.

66. This strip of paper is in the Mount Vernon collection (W-2079).

67. GW to Tobias Lear, Nov. 17, 1790, *PGWDE.*

68. GW, Cash Accounts, Nov. 16, 1771, *PGWDE.*

69. Jacob Cox Parsons, ed., *Extracts from the Diary of Jacob Hiltzheimer, of Philadelphia, 1765–1798* (Philadelphia, Press of W.F. Fell, 1893), quoted in GW, Diary, July 3, 1787, *PGWDE,* ed. note.

70. GW to Tobias Lear, June 19, 1791, *PGWDE.*

71. MW to Fanny Bassett Washington, Aug. 29, 1791, in Fields, "*Worthy Partner,*" 233.

72. "Mount Vernon Reminiscences," *Alexandria Gazette,* Jan. 18 and 22, 1876.

73. It is unclear when Sambo began using the last name Anderson. The surname does not appear in records until after his emancipation in 1801, although one of his children was named Anderson, suggesting some earlier connection to the name.

74. Sambo may be the carpenter "Sam" who appears on the 1760 list of Washington's tithable property; GW, Memorandum, List of Tithables [ca. May 1760], *PGWDE.* Earlier tax records for Washington do not survive, so we do not know when Sambo arrived at Mount Vernon. In Jan. 1760, Washington noted that "Carpenter Sam was taken with the Meazles"; Diary, Jan. 8, 1760, *PGWDE.*

75. In 1785 Washington proposed moving several of his slaves back to Mount Vernon from Ohio, where they were rented by a local tenant. He wrote to his agent, "I would make a Carpenter of Simon, to work along with his shipmate Jambo [Sambo]." Simon did not want to return, however, and the agent sold him. See GW to Thomas Freeman, Oct. 16, 1785; Freeman, "Memorandum of the Sale of the Negroes &c. at Washingtons Bottoms," Oct. 5, 1786, enc. in Freeman to GW, Dec. 18, 1786, *PGWDE,* n1.

76. Questions persist about the details of Sambo Anderson's life, specifically his age. Mount Vernon records from 1774 and 1776 refer to "a boy" named Sambo. In 1781, when seventeen Mount Vernon slaves fled to the British warship *Savage,* Washington's farm manager recorded a twenty-year-old man named Sambo among those who escaped. If the *Gazette* author's reminiscences are correct, Sambo Anderson would have been an adult by the mid-1770s and far older than twenty in 1781. However, analysis of Mount Vernon's enslaved population reveals only one individual with the name Sambo on the estate during this period, suggesting that the escapee was most likely Sambo Anderson. If this is the case, Anderson likely arrived in America later than 1750 and was younger than believed at the time of his death in 1845.

77. "Mount Vernon Reminiscences," *Alexandria Gazette*. In addition to the carved chimneypiece in the dining room, Sears is credited with suggesting the rococo pattern for the plasterwork of the dining room ceiling; GW to Lund Washington, Aug. 20, 1775; Lund Washington to GW, Nov. 12, 1775, *PGWDE.*

78. "Mount Vernon Reminiscences," *Alexandria Gazette*.

79. While the youngest three children are listed in "Washington's Slave List" of 1799 as being the children of "Sall" at River Farm, there are several reasons to believe that this attribution is an error and that these are, in fact, the children of Agnes and Sambo.

80. James Anderson to GW, Weekly Report, Jan. 27, 1798, MV Farm Accounts [photostats], Sept. 16, 1797–March 24, 1798, vol. 20-F, p. 78, Washington Library, from original manuscripts at MNHP.

81. See, for example, credit entries for July 19, 1789; July 31, 1790; June 12, 1791; Sept. 24, 1792; and Oct. 3, 1792, Ledger Book 2, folios 306R, 317R, 327R, 345R, 346R (images 610, 632, 652, 688, 690); entry for July 16, 1797, Cash Memoranda, 1794–97, p. 38.

82. Nelly Custis Lewis to Elizabeth Bordley Gibson, Feb. 23, 1823, Washington Library (A-647).

83. "Mount Vernon Reminiscences," *Alexandria Gazette*.

84. Fairfax County Court Order Books, cited on the Friends of the Freedmen's Cemetery website, accessed March 7, 2016, freedmenscemetery.org/resources/ families/documents/anderson.shtml. In the 1876 *Gazette* article, the author notes that he was part of a patrol after Nat Turner's rebellion (1831) that confiscated all firearms from African Americans in lower Fairfax County: "Among the rest I called on Uncle Sambo. The old man was loth to part with his gun; indeed, I felt sorry to take it from him, for I believe that Sambo would have shot Nat Turner could he have met him. I told the old man that I would take particular care of his gun, and use my influence to return it to him. I did return it, and never will I forget his gratitude for the same."

85. See *Alexandria Gazette*, June 12 and Dec. 21, 1810.

86. See Dorothy S. Provine, *Alexandria County, Virginia, Free Negro Registers, 1797–1861* (Bowie, MD: Heritage Books, 1990); for Charity Anderson, p. 99 (vol. 1, no. 754); for William Anderson, p. 105 (vol. 2, no. 6); for Eliza Anderson, pp. 105, 209 (vol. 2, no. 9 and vol. 3, no. 448). For manumission records for William, Eliza, and Eliza's children, see Alexandria Deed Book, Feb. 16, 1842 (B-3:282), cited on the Friends of the Freedmen's Cemetery website, accessed March 7, 2016, freedmenscemetery.org/resources/documents/manumissions.shtml.

87. *Alexandria Gazette*, Feb. 22, 1845.

88. James Anderson to GW, Weekly Report, July 7, 1798, in MV Farm Accounts [photostats], Mar. 31, 1798–Jan. 1799, vol. 20-Fa, p. 54, Washington Library, from original manuscript at MNHP.

89. Washington's team of enslaved ditchers did more than just dig ditches. They leveled earth, prepared fields, redirected waterways, and built and repaired fences.

90. See GW to John Fairfax, Mar. 31, 1789; and GW to William Pearce, May 18, 1794, *PGWDE*.

91. GW to Anthony Whitting, Dec. 16, 1792, *PGWDE*.

92. William Pearce to GW, Weekly Report, Nov. 8, 1794, GW Papers, 1741–99, Series 4: General Correspondence, 1697–1799, LOC.

93. William Pearce, credit entry for Oct. 24, 1796, MV Account Book, 1794–96, folio 80R (image 193), GW Papers, 1741–99, Series 5: Financial Papers, 1750–96, LOC.

94. GW, Last Will and Testament, July 9, 1799, *PGWDE*.

95. George Augustine Washington to GW, Apr. 8–9, 1792, *PGWDE*.

96. GW to William Pearce, Aug. 17, 1794, *PGWDE*.

97. Credit entry for Feb. 6, 1799, MV Distillery and Fishery Ledger, Washington Library (RM-297).

98. GW, Memorandum, "A Division of the Negros … of the deceasd Majr Lawrence Washington," Dec. 10, 1754, *PGWDE*.

99. GW, "Assignment of the Widow's Dower" [ca. Oct. 1759], Settlement of the Daniel Parke Custis Estate, Schedule III-A, *PGWDE*.

100. Davy's surname first appears in an entry of the MV Distillery and Fishery Ledger, in which "Davie Gray overseer" was given $7.25 on March 24, 1800, Washington Library (RM-297). It also appears on "Drafts of Negros," 1802, in which "David Gray" is listed under Nelly Parke Custis Lewis's share.

101. GW to William Pearce, Dec. 18, 1793, *PGWDE*.

102. GW to Anthony Whitting, May 26, 1793, *PGWDE*.

103. William Bowie to the Estate of Genl. George Washington, Dec. 23, 1799, Bill, Washington Library (RM-215/MS-2688).

104. Davie Gray to Mrs. Washington, Bill, Jan. 12, 1801, Peter Family Archives, Washington Library. The fact that Gray could not write suggests that unlike the hired white overseers, he did not submit a written weekly report to the plantation manager, who then compiled the information for Washington. Gray must have communicated the information in another way.

105. *Columbian Mirror and Alexandria Gazette*, Apr. 14, 1798; GW to Alexander Spotswood, Sept. 14, 1798, *PGWDE*, n1.

106. Morgan and Nicholls, "Slave Flight," 204.

107. Entry for June 3, 1799, Cash Memoranda, 1797–99, p. 96.

108. GW, "Assignment of the Widow's Dower" [ca. Oct. 1759], Settlement of the Daniel Parke Custis Estate, Schedule III-A, *PGWDE*.

109. Percentage calculated from the spouses listed on "Washington's Slave List," 1799, *PGWDE*.

110. Information transcribed from the Register of Bruton Parish Church in Williamsburg, VA, by Linda H. Rowe, historian at the Colonial Williamsburg Foundation, to Susan Fincke, Education Dept., MVLA, May 29, 1997; Mary V. Thompson Research Files, MVLA.

111. "1797. 'They Hoped They Would No Longer Be Slaves in Ten Years': Louis-Philippe," in Lee, *Experiencing Mount Vernon*, 68.

112. Credit entry, Dec. 1799, in James Anderson, MV Manager Ledger, 1798–1800, Washington Library (RM-297/MF-2915).

113. "Drafts of Negros," 1802.

114. GW to Joseph Thompson, July 2, 1766, *PGWDE*.

115. GW, Cash Accounts, Mar. 3 1767, *PGWDE*, n1.

116. Joseph Valentine to GW, Aug. 24, 1771, *PGWDE*, n1.

117. Credit entry, Dec. 3, 1791, Ledger Book 2, folio 336R (image 671).

118. GW to Anthony Whitting, Mar. 3, 1793, *PGWDE*.

119. For conditions on Caribbean sugar plantations, see Sidney W. Mintz, *Sweetness and Power: The Place of Sugar in Modern History* (New York: Penguin Books, 1985); Russell R. Menard, *Sweet Negotiations: Sugar, Slavery, and Plantation Agriculture in Early Barbados* (Charlottesville: Univ. of Virginia Press, 2006); Colleen A. Vascon-

cellos, *Slavery, Childhood, and Abolition in Jamaica, 1788–1838* (Athens: Univ. of Georgia Press, 2015).

120. Weather information from GW, Diary, Aug. 12–18, 1798, *PGWDE.*

121. James Anderson to GW, Weekly Report, Aug. 18, 1798, in MV Farm Accounts, March 31, 1798–Jan. 1799, vol. 20-Fa, p. 75, Washington Library, from original manuscript at MNHP.

122. GW to Mary Ball Washington, Feb. 15, 1787, *PGWDE.*

123. Mary Ball Washington, Will, May 29, 1788, GW Papers, 1741–97, Series 4: General Correspondence, 1697–1799, LOC.

124. Family history compiled by Ann Chinn and shared with Mount Vernon, Mar. 21, 2006; Mary V. Thompson Research Files, MVLA; Mark Auslander, "Enslaved Labor and Building the Smithsonian: Reading the Stones," *Southern Spaces*, Dec. 12, 2012, southernspaces.org/2012/enslaved-labor-and-building-smithsonian-reading-stones.

125. GW, Last Will and Testament, July 9, 1799, *PGWDE.*

126. See Scott Casper's essay, "Slavery and Freedom at Nineteenth-Century Mount Vernon," in this volume.

127. The origin of Sheels's last name is unknown. It is possible he was the son of Christopher Shade (sometimes spelled Sheldes), a hired white wagon driver who worked at Mount Vernon from December 1770 to March 1775. For references to Shade's employment, see Lund Washington, Account Book [microform], 1772–86, p. 54, Washington Library; GW, Diary, Dec. 11, 1770, *PGWDE*; entries for Christopher Shade, Ledger Book 1, folio 331L (image 781); Ledger Book 2, folio 39 (images 76–77); Ledger Book 2, folio 190R (image 379). Alce's daughter Ariana appears in only one record, from 1778. It is possible that she and Anna are the same person; GW to Lund Washington, April 22, 1778, *PGWDE.*

128. GW to Tobias Lear, Sept. 23, 1791, *PGWDE.*

129. GW to William Stoy, Oct. 14, 1797; Stoy to GW, Oct. 19, 1797, *PGWDE.*

130. GW, entry for Oct. 23, 1797, Cash Memoranda, 1797–99, p. 38.

131. GW to Roger West, Sept. 19, 1799, *PGWDE.* The note between Sheels and his wife does not survive.

132. Tobias Lear, "The last illness and Death of General Washington, Journal Account," Dec. 15, 1799, *PGWDE.*

133. Agnes Lee, *Growing Up in the 1850s: The Journal of Agnes Lee*, ed. Mary Custis Lee deButts (Chapel Hill: Univ. of North Carolina Press, 1984), 36, 80–81.

134. GW, Last Will and Testament, July 9, 1799, *PGWDE.*

135. Abigail Adams referenced Martha's fear in a letter to a friend after visiting Mount Vernon: "In the state in which they [the Washington slaves] were left by the General, to be free at her death, she did not feel as tho her Life was safe in their Hands, many of whom would be told that it was [in] their interest to get rid of her—She therefore was advised to set them all free at the close of the year"; Adams to Mary Cranch, Dec. 21, 1800, quoted in Hirschfeld, *George Washington and Slavery*, 213–14.

136. "Drafts of Negros," 1802.

137. See, for example, Anthony Whitting to GW, Jan. 15–16, 1792, *PGWDE*; William Pearce to GW, Weekly Reports, Aug. 3, 1793 and July 11, 1795, in GW Papers, 1741–97, Series 4: General Correspondence, 1697–1799, LOC; James Anderson to GW, Weekly Report, Sept. 15, 1798, MNHP; MV slavery database.

138. *Alexandria Gazette*, Nov. 16, 1835.

139. "Washington's Slave List," 1799, *PGWDE*, n7.

140. Interview of Rohulamin Quander, July 1985, in *Telling Histories: A Collection of Transcribed Interviews of Quander Family Members . . .*, ed. Rohulamin Quander (Washington, DC: Quander Historical Society, 1998), 1:3–8.

141. Gracy Quander, register no. 137 (1831) and Elizabeth Hayes, register no. 23 (1836), *Fairfax County Register of Free Blacks*, pp. 63, 113.

142. Quoted in Scott E. Casper, *Sarah Johnson's Mount Vernon: The Forgotten History of an American Shrine* (New York: Hill and Wang, 2008), 196. Details of Parker's life and Mount Vernon in the nineteenth century have been drawn from this work.

143. Casper, *Sarah Johnson's Mount Vernon.*, 185.

144. "Guardian of the Dead," *Washington Post*, Nov. 18, 1894, quoted in Casper, *Sarah Johnson's Mount Vernon*, 186.

145. Mrs. J. L. Holbrook, "Seven Days at Our National Capital," *The International: An Illustrated Monthly Magazine of Travel and Literature* 5, no. 4 (Oct. 1898): 279.

146. *Washington Post*, Dec. 31, 1898 (obituary); *New York Sun*, Jan. 15, 1899 ("Faithful Guardian"), quoted in Casper, *Sarah Johnson's Mount Vernon*, 197.

147. Harrison Howell Dodge to Justine Van Rensselaer Townsend, Aug. 5, 1898, quoted in Casper, *Sarah Johnson's Mount Vernon*, 198.

148. Casper, *Sarah Johnson's Mount Vernon*, 225. At least one of Parker's children carried on the family tradition of serving in prominent American institutions. After several years joining his father at Mount Vernon, Parker's son Harry was hired to work a variety of jobs at the U.S. Capitol. In the late 1880s, he was appointed as an assistant for the House Ways and Means Committee, preparing for meetings, serving as doorkeeper, and tending to committee members' needs. When Harry retired in 1937, the House voted to supply him with an annual pension of $1,260. One congressman described Harry as being "as much a part of this institution as is the dome over this building"; "Harry Needs a Rest," *History, Art & Archives of the United States House of Representatives* (blog), Sept. 29, 2014, history.house.gov/Blog/Detail/15032407924.

GEORGE WASHINGTON AND SLAVERY

1. Philip J. Schwarz, ed., *Slavery at the Home of George Washington* (Mount Vernon, VA: MVLA, 2001), 1. Citations will be primarily for quotations.

2. Philip D. Morgan, "'To Get Quit of Negroes': George Washington and Slavery," *Journal of American Studies* 39, no. 3 (Dec. 2005), 403–29; L. Scott Philyaw, "Washington and Slavery," in *A Companion to George Washington*, ed. Edward G. Lengel (Malden, MA: Wiley-Blackwell, 2012), 104–20.

3. Jackson T. Main, "The One Hundred," *WMQ*, 3d Ser., 11, no. 3 (1954), 354–84 (in 1787–88 GW paid tax on 390 slaves: 352 in Fairfax, 27 in Berkeley, and 11 in Stafford Counties respectively); GW to John Augustine Washington, June 14, 1755, *PGWDE* (Clio); GW to Anthony Whitting, Nov. 11, 1792, *PGWDE* (steadily); GW to Whitting, Nov. 18 and 25, 1792, *PGWDE* (villainies); GW to John Francis Mercer, Dec. 5, 1786, *PGWDE* (property); Philip D. Morgan and Michael L. Nicholls, "Slave Flight: Mount Vernon, Virginia, and the Wider Atlantic World," in *George Washington's South*, ed. Tamara Harvey and Greg O'Brien (Gainesville: Univ. Press of Florida, 2004), 197–222.

4. GW to William Pearce, Dec. 18, 1793, *PGWDE* (Davy).

5. Lorena S. Walsh, "Slavery and Agriculture at Mount Vernon," in Schwarz, *Slavery*, 47–77. For the first recognition that he had too many slaves, see GW to John Posey, June 11, 1769, *PGWDE*. GW's slaves at Mount Vernon grew some tobacco during the Revolutionary War and in the 1780s.

6. Philyaw, "Washington and Slavery," 104; GW to Bryan Fairfax, Aug. 24, 1774, *PGWDE*; Rosemarie Zagarri, ed., *David Humphreys' "Life of General Washington with George Washington's Remarks"* (Athens: Univ. of Georgia Press, 1991), 6.

7. Phillis Wheatley to GW, Oct. 26, 1775; GW to Wheatley, Feb. 28, 1776; GW to Lund Washington, Aug. 15, 1778, *PGWDE*.

8. GW to Robert Morris, Apr. 12, 1786; GW to Lafayette, May 10, 1786; GW to John Francis Mercer, Sept. 9, 1786, *PGWDE*. For Washington's abolitionist readings, see François Furstenberg, "Atlantic Slavery, Atlantic Freedom: George Washington, Slavery, and Transatlantic Abolitionist Networks," *WMQ*, 3d Ser., 68, no. 2 (2011): 247–86.

9. For a sampling, see GW to Arthur Young, Dec. 12, 1793, *PGWDE*; GW to Tobias Lear, May 6, 1794, *PGWDE*, n13; GW to Alexander Spotswood, Nov. 23, 1794, *PGWDE*; GW to William Pearce, Jan. 27, 1796, *WGW*, 34:427; and GW to David Stuart, Feb. 7, 1796, *WGW*, 34:452–53.

10. GW, Last Will and Testament, July 9, 1799, *PGWDE*; Patricia Brady, *Martha Washington: An American Life* (New York: Viking, 2005), 225. In addition to works previously cited, the key works on Washington and slavery are Fritz Hirschfeld, ed., *George Washington and Slavery: A Documentary Portrayal* (Columbia: Univ. of Missouri Press, 1997); Kenneth Morgan, "George Washington and the Problem of Slavery," *Journal of American Studies* 34 (2000): 279–301; Dorothy Twohig, "'That Species of Property': Washington's Role in the Controversy over Slavery," in *George Washington Reconsidered*, ed. Don Higginbotham (Charlottesville: Univ. Press of Virginia, 2001), 114–38; Henry Wiencek, *An Imperfect God: George Washington, His Slaves, and the Creation of America* (New York: Farrar, Straus and Giroux, 2003); and Peter R. Henriques, *Realistic Visionary: A Portrait of George Washington* (Charlottesville: Univ. of Virginia Press, 2006), esp. 145–65. For excellent biographies that give considerable attention to slavery, see Joseph J. Ellis, *His Excellency: George Washington* (New York: Alfred A. Knopf, 2004); Ron Chernow, *Washington: A Life* (New York: Penguin Press, 2010); and Robert Middlekauf, *Washington's Revolution: The Making of America's First Leader* (New York: Alfred A. Knopf, 2015).

RESISTING ENSLAVEMENT

1. See, for example, Gerald W. Mullin, *Flight and Rebellion: Slave Resistance in Eighteenth-Century Virginia* (London: Oxford Univ. Press, 1975).

2. GW to William Pearce, Jan. 12, 1794, *PGWDE*.

3. GW to Gov. Henry Lee, Oct. 16, 1793, *PGWDE*.

4. GW to William Pearce, Feb. 22, 1795, *PGWDE*.

5. GW to William Pearce, Oct. 6, 1793, *PGWDE*; GW to Anthony Whitting, Oct. 14, 1792, *PGWDE*; GW to James Anderson, Jan. 22, 1797, Washington Library.

6. GW to Anthony Whitting, Feb. 3 and 17, 1793, *PGWDE*.

7. GW, Diary, Mar. 8, 1787, *PGWDE*.

8. James Bloxham to Mr. [William] Peacy, July 23, 1786, typescript, Washington

Library. For an earlier conspiracy to poison their overseers by eight slaves in the area, see *Pennsylvania Gazette*, Dec. 31, 1767, as quoted in GW to John Posey, June 11, 1769, *PGWDE*, n4.

9. Philip D. Morgan and Michael L. Nicholls, "Slave Flight: Mount Vernon, Virginia, and the Wider Atlantic World," in *George Washington's South*, ed. Tamara Harvey and Greg O'Brien (Gainesville: Univ. Press of Florida, 2004), 203–4, 206, 208–13. On barriers to female slaves escaping, see Annette Gordon-Reed, *The Hemingses of Monticello: An American Family* (New York: W. W. Norton, 2008), 412–13.

10. Lund Washington to GW, Dec. 3, 1775, *PGWDE*.

11. Lund Washington, List of Runaways, Apr. 1781, in *WGW*, 22:14n; for another published version of this list, which differs slightly, see [Ellen McCallister Clark], "A Wartime Incident," in *Annual Report 1986* (Mount Vernon, VA: MVLA, 1987), 25. On escaped Washington and Custis slaves dying of disease, see John Parke Custis to Martha Washington, Oct. 12, 1781, in Joseph E. Fields, *"Worthy Partner": The Papers of Martha Washington* (Westport, CT: Greenwood Press, 1994), 187. On former Mount Vernon slaves going to Canada with the British (and even to Sierra Leone), see Simon Schama, *Rough Crossings: Britain, the Slaves, and the American Revolution* (London: BBC Books, 2005), 148–49, 232, 281, 381, 383.

"ANXIOUS FOR THE WEEKLY REMARKS"

1. "Project History," The Papers of George Washington, accessed Aug. 18, 2015, gwpapers.virginia.edu/about/project-history-awards.

2. For the slaves inherited by George Washington from his father and older half-brother, see Worthington Chauncey Ford, ed., *Wills of George Washington and His Immediate Ancestors* (Brooklyn, NY: Historical Printing Club, 1891), 42, 42n; GW, Memorandum, "1st Division of part of my dec'd Brothr Lawrences Negroes . . ." [1754], Division of Slaves, Dec. 10, 1754, III, *PGWDE*; GW, Cash Accounts, 1761, *PGWDE*, n60; GW, Memorandum, Division of Slaves [1762], *PGWDE*.

3. Joseph E. Fields, *"Worthy Partner": The Papers of Martha Washington* (Westport, CT: Greenwood Press, 1994), 61–75, 105–7, 126, 132–34; Advertisement for Runaway Slaves, Aug. 11, 1761, *PGWDE*, n5 (printed in the *Maryland Gazette* [Annapolis], Aug. 20, 1761); Joseph Valentine to GW, Nov. 21, 1770, *PGWDE*, n2.

4. For slaves purchased by Washington following his marriage (at least 15 in 1759; an unknown number in 1761; 10 in 1762; 13 in 1764; 5 in 1767; 2 in 1770; 1 in 1771; 3 in 1772; 4 in 1773; and 2 in 1775), see *PGW: Colonial Series*, 6:198, 200n15, 313, 314n3, 314n4, 321, 321n8; 7:4, 9n67, 62, 66, 106, 109, 110, 299, 300n17, 304–5, 336–7, 469; 8:41, 42n, 82, 83n, 347n, 532n; 9:35, 36n, 222, 224n, 239n, 505n; 10:269, 269n, 303, 304n, 319n.

5. *PGW: Colonial Series*, 6:428; 7:45, 139, 227–28, 313, 376–77, 442–43, 515–16; 8:104, 220–21, 356–57, 479; 9:54–55, 238–39; 10:135.

6. GW, Memorandum, List of Tithables, June 4, 1761; July 1774, *PGWDE*.

7. For the 1786 list, see GW, Diary, Feb. 18, 1786, *PGWDE*; the 1799 Mount Vernon slave list and a list of slaves rented from Mrs. Penelope French can be found in "Washington's Slave List," 1799, *PGWDE*.

8. GW to George Augustine Washington, May 17, 1787, *PGWDE*.

9. For an example of a weekly report, see Farm Reports [August 16–22, 1789], *PGWDE*.

10. For two of the best visitor descriptions, see Louis-Philippe, *Diary of My Travels in America*, trans. Stephen Becker (New York, NY: Delacorte, 1977), 31–32; and Julian Ursyn Niemcewicz, *Under Their Vine and Fig Tree: Travels through America in 1797–1799, 1805*, ed. and trans. Metchie J. E. Budka (Elizabeth, NJ: Grassmann, 1965), 97, 99–101, 103, 106. For two rare interviews with Martha Washington's maid, Oney Judge, who escaped during the presidency, see Benjamin Chase, "Mrs. [?] Staines," in *Slave Testimony: Two Centuries of Letters, Speeches, Interviews, and Autobiographies*, ed. John W. Blassingame (Baton Rouge: Louisiana State Univ. Press, 1977), 248–50; and T. H. Adams, "Washington's Runaway Slave, and How Portsmouth Freed Her," in *Frank W. Miller's Portsmouth, New Hampshire, Weekly*, June 2, 1877 (reprinted from the *Granite Freeman*, May 22, 1845).

11. For free black registers, see Dorothy S. Provine, *Alexandria County, Virginia, Free Negro Registers, 1797–1861* (Bowie, MD: Heritage Books, 1990); Dorothy S. Provine, *District of Columbia Free Negro Registers, 1821–1861*, 2 vols. (Bowie, MD: Heritage Books, 1996); and *Fairfax County Register of Free Blacks*. For descendants of Mount Vernon slaves purchasing land, see Paula Elsey, "Another Day on Harley Road," *South County Chronicle* 4, no. 10 (Nov. 1, 2004): 1–5 (Fairfax County Public Library, Virginia Room, Fairfax, VA).

THE TINIEST OF DETAILS

1. The project encompasses documents that provide information about not only those who worked at Mount Vernon (regardless of ownership) but also individuals related in some way (usually by marriage) to the enslaved at Mount Vernon as well as those who lived at the many properties owned by George Washington or the Custis estate. By expanding beyond Mount Vernon references, the project hopes to identify the larger interplantation network of the enslaved community.

2. On the House for Families excavation, see Eleanor Breen's essay, "The Archaeology of Enslavement," in this volume.

3. GW, Diary, Feb. 18, 1786, and "Washington's Slave List," 1799, *PGWDE*.

4. The database contains 26 different spellings of Breechy between 1757 and 1799.

5. To distinguish among individuals, the digital humanities database team assigned each person a consistently spelled name followed by an alpha character designation (e.g., A, B, C), especially helpful for individuals with the same name (e.g., Jack or Will). As of March 2016, we identified 942 individuals, with 540 of them residing at Mount Vernon.

6. Lund Washington, Account Book [microform], 1772–86, p. 55, Washington Library.

7. GW, Diary, July 5–9, 1763, *PGWDE*.

8. Credit entry for May 13, 1795, William Pearce, Mount Vernon Account Book, 1794–96, folio 32R (image 102), GW Papers, 1741–99: Series 5: Financial Papers, 1750–96, LOC.

9. GW, "Assignment of the Widow's Dower" [ca. Oct. 1759] and "List of Artisans and Household Slaves in the Estate" [ca. 1759], Settlement of the Daniel Parke Custis Estate, Schedules III-A, III-C, *PGWDE*.

10. GW, Memorandum, List of Tithables and Taxable Land and Property [ca. June 16, 1766], *PGWDE*. For the purchase of Hannah and her child, see credit entry, June 16, 1759, Ledger Book 1, folio 56R (image 156).

11. Credit entry, June 7, 1779, Ledger Book 1, folio 302R, (image 710).

12. GW, Diary, Oct. 22, 1761; Jul. 5–9, 1763, *PGWDE*; debit entries, Ledger Book 1, folio 185L (image 445).

13. GW, Diary, Oct. 19, 1765, *PGWDE*.

THE ARCHAEOLOGY OF ENSLAVEMENT

1. Julian Ursyn Niemcewicz, "1798. Acute Observations: From Domestic Pursuits to Concern for the Nation," in *Experiencing Mount Vernon: Eyewitness Accounts, 1784–1865*, ed. Jean B. Lee (Charlottesville: Univ. of Virginia Press, 2006), 77, 79.

2. Leslie King-Hammond, "Identifying Spaces of Blackness: The Aesthetics of Resistance and Identity in American Plantation Art," in *Landscapes of Slavery: The Plantation in American Art*, ed. Angela D. Mack and Stephen G. Hoffius (Columbia: Univ. of South Carolina Press, 2008), 58–85.

3. Patricia Samford, "The Archaeology of African-American Slavery and Material Culture," *WMQ*, 3d Ser., 53, no. 1 (January 1996): 87–114; Theresa A. Singleton, ed., *'I, Too, Am America': Archaeological Studies of African-American Life* (Charlottesville: Univ. of Virginia Press, 1999).

4. Dennis J. Pogue, "Slave Lifeways at Mount Vernon: An Archaeological Perspective," in *Slavery at the Home of George Washington*, ed. Philip J. Schwarz (Mount Vernon, VA: MVLA, 2001), 111–35; Pogue, "The Domestic Architecture of Slavery at George Washington's Mount Vernon," *Winterthur Portfolio* 37, no. 1 (Spring 2002): 3–22.

5. Dennis J. Pogue, "Mount Vernon Archaeology: Program Description," Archaeology Department, MVLA, 1991.

6. Joanne Bowen, "Faunal Remains from the House for Families Cellar (44FX762/47)," report to MVLA, 1993; Pogue, "Slave Lifeways," 117–21; Joanne Bowen and Susan Trevarthen Andrews, with contributions by Stephen Atkins and Dessa Lightfoot, "Faunal Analysis for Mount Vernon," report for George Washington's Mount Vernon Archaeology Division, MVLA, 2016.

7. Bowen, "Faunal Remains"; Stephen C. Atkins, "An Archaeological Perspective on the African-American Slave Diet at Mount Vernon's House for Families" (master's thesis, College of William and Mary, 1994).

8. Joanne Bowen, "Foodways in the 18th-Century Chesapeake," in *The Archaeology of 18th-Century Virginia*, ed. Theodore R. Reinhart (Richmond, VA: Spectrum Press, 1996), 87–130; Samford, "Archaeology of African-American Slavery," 95–97; Maria Franklin, "An Archaeological Study of the Rich Neck Slave Quarter and Enslaved Domestic Life," Colonial Williamsburg Research Publications (Williamsburg, VA: Colonial Williamsburg Foundation, 2004).

9. Justine W. McKnight, "A Study of the Macro-botanical Remains Recovered from the House for Families at George Washington's Mount Vernon, 44FX762/40 and 44FX762/47," report for George Washington's Mount Vernon Archaeology Division, MVLA, 2015.

10. Stephen A. Mrozowski, Maria Franklin, and Leslie Hunt, "Archaeobotanical Analysis and Interpretations of Enslaved Virginian Plant Use at Rich Neck Plantation," *American Antiquity* 73, no. 4 (Oct. 2008): 699–728.

11. Dot, diaper, and basket pattern plates made up only 12 percent of the total salt-glazed stoneware assemblage from the midden site, compared to one-third of the assemblage from the House for Families; Pogue, "Slave Lifeways," 113–17.

12. Robert Cary & Co., London, to GW, Invoice, Mar. 31 1761; Apr. 23, 1763; Dec. 3, 1771; GW to Robert Cary & Co., Invoice, Nov. 15, 1762, *PGWDE.*

13. Jillian E. Galle, "Strategic Consumption: Archaeological Evidence for Costly Signaling among Enslaved Men and Women in the Eighteenth-Century Chesapeake" (PhD diss., Univ. of Virginia, 2006).

14. References to such purchases appear frequently in Washington's papers and are being compiled in the Mount Vernon slavery database, described in Molly Kerr's essay, "The Tiniest of Details," in this volume.

15. GW to Robert Cary & Co., Invoice, July 15, 1772; Robert Cary & Co., to GW, Invoice, Sept. 29, 1772, *PGWDE.*

16. Colonoware has also been recovered in smaller amounts around Mount Vernon outbuildings like the blacksmith's shop, the kitchen, and an early wash house.

17. Barbara Heath, "Temper, Temper: Recent Scholarship on Colonoware in 18th-Century Virginia," in Reinhart, *Archaeology of 18th-Century Virginia,* 149–76; Samford, "Archaeology of African-American Slavery," 102–3; Andrew S. Veech, "Considering Colonoware from the Barnes Plantation: A Proposed Colonoware Typology for Northern Virginia Colonial Sites," *Northeast Historical Archaeology* 26, no. 1 (1997): 73–86; Daniel L. Mouer et al., "Colonoware Pottery, Chesapeake Pipes, and 'Uncritical Assumptions,'" in Singleton, *'I, Too, Am America,'* 83–115; Eleanor E. Breen, "Whose Trash Is It, Anyway? A Stratigraphic and Ceramic Analysis of the South Grove Midden (44FX762/17), Mount Vernon, Virginia," *Northeast Historical Archaeology* 33, no. 1 (2004): 111–30.

18. Bruce W. Bevan, "A Geophysical Survey at Mount Vernon," unpublished report to the MVLA, 1985; Joseph A. Downer, "Hallowed Ground, Sacred Place: The Slave Cemetery at George Washington's Mount Vernon and the Cultural Landscape of the Enslaved" (master's thesis, George Washington Univ., 2015).

THE LANDSCAPE OF ENSLAVEMENT

1. GW, Diary, Apr. 8, 1760, *PGWDE.*

2. GW, "Assignment of the Widow's Dower" [ca. Oct. 1759], Settlement of the Daniel Parke Custis Estate, Schedule III-A, *PGWDE.*

3. Barbara Heath, "Space and Place within Plantation Quarters in Virginia, 1700–1825," in *Cabin, Quarter, Plantation: Architecture and Landscapes of North American Slavery,* ed. Clifton Ellis and Rebecca Ginsburg (New Haven: Yale Univ. Press, 2010), 156–76; Garrett Fesler, "Excavating the Spaces and Interpreting the Places of Enslaved Africans," in Ellis and Ginsburg, *Cabin, Quarter, Plantation,* 27–50.

4. GW, "A plan of my farm on Little Huntg. Creek & Potomk. R.," 1766, Geography and Map Division, LOC, hdl.loc.gov/loc.gmd/g3882m.ct000085.

5. GW, "Farms and their contents," Dec. 1793, Huntington Library, San Marino, CA; gwpapers.virginia.edu/documents_gw/maps/farm/plain.html. On agricultural practices, see Jean B. Lee, "Mount Vernon Plantation: A Model for the Republic," in *Slavery at the Home of George Washington,* ed. Philip J. Schwarz (Mount Vernon, VA: MVLA, 2001), 12–45.

6. GW, Memorandum [June 1791], *PGWDE.* Washington had combined Ferry's and French's plantations into Union Farm as early as 1788, although they retained their separate identities for several more years.

7. GW to William Pearce, Dec. 23, 1793, *PGWDE.*

8. GW to William Pearce, June 7, 1793, *WGW*, 34:212.

9. GW to Anthony Whitting, Feb. 24, 1793; GW to William Pearce, Dec. 23, 1793, *PGWDE*.

10. Dennis J. Pogue, "The Domestic Architecture of Slavery at George Washington's Mount Vernon," *Winterthur Portfolio* 37, no. 1 (Spring 2002): 3–22.

11. Advertisement, "To be Let …" *Columbian Mirror and Alexandrian Gazette*, Feb. 27, 1796, *WGW*, 34:434.

12. GW to William Pearce, Dec. 18, 1793, *PGWDE*.

13. Pogue, "Domestic Architecture of Slavery."

14. Samuel Vaughan, Presentation Drawing of Mount Vernon, 1787, MVLA (W-1434).

15. GW to Samuel Vaughan, Nov. 12, 1787, *PGWDE*.

16. GW to William Pearce, Dec. 23, 1793, *PGWDE*.

SLAVERY AND FREEDOM AT NINETEENTH-CENTURY
MOUNT VERNON

1. These sources provide the foundation for Scott E. Casper, *Sarah Johnson's Mount Vernon: The Forgotten History of an American Shrine* (New York: Hill and Wang, 2008), from which the history in this essay is drawn. In this essay I cite sources only of direct quotations.

2. When possible, I include dates of birth and death for individuals for whom the reader would not otherwise be able to procure this information. In addition, including these dates indicates for these enslaved (and in some cases later emancipated) individuals the sort of historical significance that is typically attached to more prominent figures. The key source for Bushrod's enslaved population is his "List of my Negroes, July 24, 1815" and "Meal Allowance for 1814," in John Augustine Washington III, Mount Vernon Farm Book, MVLA Archives, Washington Library. For Mount Vernon's enslaved population of the 1840s and 1850s, the diaries of John Augustine Washington III, also in the MVLA Archives, are an essential source, because he typically listed his enslaved people and their birth dates in the front pages.

3. For discussion of the African Americans freed by the terms of Washington's will, see Edna Greene Medford, "Beyond Mount Vernon: George Washington's Emancipated Laborers and Their Descendants," in *Slavery at the Home of George Washington*, ed. Philip J. Schwarz (Mount Vernon, VA: MVLA, 2001), 136–57.

4. See Jean B. Lee, "Jane C. Washington, Family, and Nation at Mount Vernon, 1830–1855," in *Women Shaping the South: Creating and Confronting Change*, ed. Angela Boswell and Judith N. McArthur (Columbia: Univ. of Missouri Press, 2006), 30–49.

5. Caroline Healey (Dall) Journals, June 10, 1843 (reel 33), Massachusetts Historical Society.

6. Horace Greeley, "Playing on the Bones," *New York Tribune*, Jan. 1859, reprinted in *Liberator* 29 (Jan. 14, 1859): 1.

PICTURING GEORGE WASHINGTON, MOUNT VERNON,
AND SLAVERY

1. John C. Calhoun was one of the first politicians and proslavery defenders to use the term *positive good* in defense of slavery. In a speech to Congress in 1837, Calhoun argued that slavery was not an evil but a "positive good," "indispensable to the peace

and happiness of both" black and white people. For further discussion of mid-nine-teenth century representations of George Washington and Mount Vernon, see Maurie D. McInnis, "The Most Famous Plantation of All: The Politics of Painting Mount Vernon," in *Landscapes of Slavery: The Plantation in American Art*, ed. Angela D. Mack and Stephen G. Hoffius (Columbia: Univ. of South Carolina Press, 2008), 86-114.

2. Three of the paintings are in the collection of the Virginia Museum of the Fine Arts, Richmond: *The Marriage of Washington* (1849); *Washington as a Captain in the French and Indian War* (1851); and *Washington as a Farmer, at Mount Vernon* (1851). The fourth, *Washington on His Deathbed* (1851), is owned by the Dayton Institute of Art, Dayton, Ohio. *Washington as Statesman, at the Constitutional Convention* (1856), also at the Virginia Museum of the Fine Arts, appears to be a later addition to the series. *Washington as a Farmer* was exhibited at the National Academy of Design (1854), Pennsylvania Academy of the Fine Arts (1854), and Fine Arts Institute, New York (1863). According to Stearns's obituary, "These pictures were lithographed and the artist received a large royalty from their estate"; "The Death of J. B. Stearns," *New York Times*, Sept. 19, 1885, 1. My thanks to Elizabeth O'Leary for this citation.

3. Stearns was likely guided in his depiction by George Washington Parke Custis, the grandson of Martha Washington, who was unofficially adopted by the first president and raised at Mount Vernon. Stearns visited with Custis at his plantation, Arlington House, where Custis had preserved a treasury of Washington heirlooms.

4. Mignot was from a slaveholding family in Charleston, South Carolina, and during the Civil War was known to be a supporter of the Confederacy. The idea of the painting may well have been inspired by a 1784 letter from Lafayette to Washington only recently published in the Dec. 11, 1857, *New York Daily Times*, in which the marquis spoke of his plan to leave Philadelphia shortly because "there is no rest for me until I go to Mount Vernon. I long for the pleasure to embrace you, my dear General, and the happiness of being once more with you will be so great that no words can ever express it"; T. P. Rossiter, *A Description of the Picture of the Home of Washington after the War: Painted by T. P. Rossiter and L. R. Mignot, with Historical Sketches of the Personages Introduced* (New York: D. Appleton, 1859), 3, 5. Rossiter also published an article on Mount Vernon in which he wrote of his visit to the estate and his imaginings and recollections of history; Thomas P. Rossiter, "Mount Vernon, Past and Present. What Shall Be Its Destiny?" *Crayon* 5 (Sept. 1858), 243–53. His descriptions of both Washington's biography and slavery are highly romanticized.

5. GW to Anthony Whitting, Jan. 6, 1793, quoted in Jean B. Lee, "Mount Vernon Plantation: A Model for the Republic," in *Slavery at the Home of George Washington*, ed. Philip J. Schwarz (Mount Vernon, VA: MVLA, 2001), 24. For more on slavery at Mount Vernon, see Henry Wiencek, *An Imperfect God: George Washington, His Slaves, and the Creation of America* (New York: Farrar, Straus and Giroux, 2003); and Lee, "Mount Vernon Plantation," 13–45.

6. "Mount Vernon," *New York Daily Times*, July 4, 1853, 2. For nineteenth-century visitors, it was both the Mansion House and the tomb that held special symbolic force.

7. Benjamin Brown French, Diary, May 23, 1834, in *Experiencing Mount Vernon: Eyewitness Accounts, 1784–1865*, ed. Jean B. Lee (Charlottesville: Univ. of Virginia Press, 2006), 143.

8. "List of slaves belonging to John A. Washington [III], Mount Vernon, January 15, 1856," taken from his diary, Washington Library; quoted in Patricia Hills, "Painting Race: Eastman Johnson's Pictures of Slaves, Ex-Slaves, and Freedmen," in *Eastman Johnson: Painting America*, ed. Teresa A. Carbone and Patricia Hills (New York: Brooklyn Museum of Art in association with Rizzoli, 1999), 160. "The Slaves of Mr. Custis," *New York Daily Times*, Dec. 30, 1857. The term *slave pen* had a pointed period meaning that referred to the holding places used by slave traders.

9. The doorway depicted by Johnson does not appear in the earliest view of Mount Vernon and is not part of the building today. It could have been cut in by a subsequent owner and later covered over. We do not know, therefore, whether Johnson added it for pictorial effect or whether he made an accurate sketch of the architectural arrangement he saw in 1857. George Washington designated this building as a "servant's hall," and it was used to lodge (white) servants of guests during their stay. It mirrors the building on the other side of the house that was used as the kitchen during Washington's life.

10. On the internal slave trade, see Maurie D. McInnis, *Slaves Waiting for Sale: Abolitionist Art and the American Slave Trade* (Chicago: Univ. of Chicago Press, 2011).

Further Readings

Baumgarten, Linda. "'Clothes for the People': Slave Clothing in Early Virginia." *Journal of Early Southern Decorative Arts* 14, no. 2 (Nov. 1988): 27–70.

Berlin, Ira. *Many Thousands Gone: The First Two Centuries of Slavery in North America*. Cambridge, MA: Harvard University Press, 2000.

Breen, Eleanor. "The revolution before the Revolution? A Material Culture Approach to Consumerism at George Washington's Mount Vernon, VA." PhD diss., University of Tennessee, Knoxville, 2013.

Casper, Scott E. *Sarah Johnson's Mount Vernon: The Forgotten History of an American Shrine*. New York: Hill & Wang, 2008.

Ellis, Joseph J. *His Excellency: George Washington*. New York: Vintage, 2005.

Furstenberg, François. "Atlantic Slavery, Atlantic Freedom: George Washington, Slavery, and Transatlantic Abolitionist Networks." The *William and Mary Quarterly*, 3d Ser., 68, no. 2 (Apr. 2011): 247–86.

Genovese, Eugene. *Roll, Jordon, Roll: The World the Slaves Made*. New York: Vintage, 1976.

Hirschfeld, Fritz. *George Washington and Slavery: A Documentary Portrayal*. Columbia: University of Missouri Press, 1997.

McInnis, Maurie D. "The Most Famous Plantation of All: The Politics of Painting Mount Vernon." In Angela D. Mack and Stephen G. Hoffius, eds. *Landscape of Slavery: The Plantation in American Art*. Columbia: University of South Carolina Press, 2008, 86–109.

Morgan, Kenneth. "George Washington and the Problem of Slavery." *Journal of American Studies* 34, no. 2 (Aug. 2000): 279–301.

Morgan, Philip D. *Slave Counterpoint: Black Culture in the Eighteenth-Century Chesapeake and Lowcountry*. Chapel Hill: University of North Carolina Press, 1998.

Morgan, Philip D. "'To Get Quit of Negroes': George Washington and Slavery." *Journal of American Studies* 39, no. 3 (Dec. 2005): 403–29.

Morgan, Philip D. and Michael L. Nicholls. "Slave Flight: Mount Vernon, Virginia, and the Wider Atlantic World." In Tamara Harvey and Greg O'Brien, eds. *George Washington's South*. Gainesville: University Press of Florida, 2004, 197–222.

Pogue, Dennis J. "Interpreting the Dimensions of Daily Life for the Slaves Living at the President's House and at Mount Vernon." *Pennsylvania Magazine of History and Biography* 129, no. 4 (Oct. 2005): 433–43.

Pogue, Dennis J. "The Domestic Architecture of Slavery at George Washington's Mount Vernon." *Winterthur Portfolio* 37, no. 1 (Spring 2002): 3–22.

Schwarz, Philip J., ed. *Slavery at the Home of George Washington*. Mount Vernon, VA: Mount Vernon Ladies' Association, 2001.

Waldstreicher, David. *Slavery's Constitution: From Revolution to Ratification.* New York: Hill & Wang, 2009.

Wiencek, Henry. *An Imperfect God: George Washington, His Slaves, and the Creation of America*. New York: Farrar, Straus and Giroux, 2003.

Contributors

ELEANOR BREEN is a historical archaeologist with two decades experience on plantation sites in the mid-Atlantic region. Currently, Eleanor is part of Alexandria Archaeology, which preserves and interprets the City of Alexandria, Virginia's history. Eleanor holds three degrees in anthropology, a BA from the College of William and Mary, an MA from the University of Massachusetts Boston, and a PhD from the University of Tennessee, Knoxville. Her research interests include material culture research, the consumer revolution, and the archaeology of enslavement.

SCOTT E. CASPER is the author of *Sarah Johnson's Mount Vernon: The Forgotten History of an American Shrine* (2008) and has written or edited eight other books. He is the dean of the College of Arts, Humanities, and Social Sciences and professor of history at the University of Maryland, Baltimore County. Since 2000 he has worked extensively with the education department of George Washington's Mount Vernon, providing presentations and workshops for K-12 teachers on site and around the United States.

ANNETTE GORDON-REED is the Charles Warren Professor of American Legal History at Harvard Law School, Professor of History in the Faculty of Arts and Sciences, and the Carol K. Pforzheimer Professor at the Radcliffe Institute for Advanced Study at Harvard University. She is the author of five books and the editor of one volume. She won the 2008 National Book Award for General Non-Fiction and the 2009 Pulitzer Prize for History for *The Hemingses of Monticello: An American Family*. Gordon-Reed has received numerous fellowships and awards, including Guggenheim and MacArthur fellowships and a 2009 National Humanities Medal.

The late GLORIA TANCIL HOLMES was a member of the Quander family, with ancestry tracing back to Suckey Bay, an enslaved fieldworker on Mount Vernon's River Farm. Holmes was the daughter of Gladys Quander Tancil, the first African American historical interpreter at Mount Vernon.

MOLLY H. KERR holds an MA in anthropology from the University of Arkansas-Fayetteville and a BA in anthropology from the University of Mary Washington. From 2013 to 2016, Molly served as the Digital Humanities Project Manager at Mount Vernon, where she managed the slavery database and coordinated efforts to catalog Washington's world of objects, landscape, plants, and animals.

JESSIE MACLEOD is an associate curator at George Washington's Mount Vernon and lead curator for the exhibition, "Lives Bound Together: Slavery at George Washington's Mount Vernon," opening in 2016. Jessie received a BA in history from Yale University and an MA in history, with a certificate in public history, from the University of Massachusetts Amherst. Prior to coming to Mount Vernon as assistant curator in 2012, she worked at James Madison's Montpelier, the Newport Historical Society, the New Haven Museum, Historic Deerfield, and the Yale University Art Gallery. Her research interests include African American history, early American women's history, and material culture.

MAURIE D. MCINNIS is professor of art history and executive vice president and provost at the University of Texas at Austin. She is the author of *Slaves Waiting for Sale: Abolitionist Art and the American Slave Trade* (2011) and curator of the 2015 Library of Virginia exhibition, "To Be Sold: Virginia and the American Slave Trade."

ZSUN-NEE MILLER-MATEMA is a cultural artist and social advocate. She is the president of the Washington, Custis-Lee Enslaved Remembrance Society, a virtual descendants' collective sharing genealogies, stories and concerns of family ties and bonds with Founding Fathers and Mothers. She holds a BA in psychology and an MSc in Holistic Counseling. She is a writer, past host and producer for XM Satellite, Radio One and Cable. Her interest in researching history, transformational therapies, lectures and performances are testimony to her life's work in intercultural relations. As a descendant of Caroline Branham, personal maid to Martha Washington, she has contributed articles to historical publications and the End Note for the National Geographic publication, *Master George's People*. She is a mother of 4 daughters, 13 grandchildren and 2 great-great grandchildren. She is currently writing the children's book, *Why Slavery*, a discovery for young readers into the reasons and circumstances of African enslavement.

PHILIP D. MORGAN is Harry C. Black Professor of History at The Johns Hopkins University. He has been interested in eighteenth-century slavery and plantation life for longer than he cares to remember. George Washington's involvement in slavery and attempt to extricate himself from the institution's embrace has long intrigued him, but now he is at work trying to reconstruct the enslaved community at Mount Vernon. He hopes to illuminate the lived experience of slavery, its messy realities, and the entanglements to which it gave rise.

ROHULAMIN QUANDER is a retired senior administrative law judge for the District of Columbia. He is founder and president of the Quander Historical Society, Inc., established in 1985 to research, preserve, educate, and share the history of the Quander Family. In 1984, Judge Quander chaired the Quander Tricentennial Celebration, 1684–1984, to celebrate 300 documented years in America. Further documentation has established the Quander presence from the 1670s in the local Maryland-Virginia region. One of the oldest African American families in the United States, Quander ancestors were enslaved at Mount Vernon, and trace their Mount Vernon legacy to Suckey Bay (mother of Nancy Carter Quander), West Ford, and Tobias Lear.

SUSAN P. SCHOELWER is the Robert H. Smith Senior Curator at George Washington's Mount Vernon, where she has directed the refurnishing and reinterpretation of the "New Room," the reinstallation of the greenhouse slave quarter, and numerous other room furnishing projects and exhibitions. She holds a PhD in American studies from Yale University, an MA from the Winterthur Program at the University of Delaware, and a BA in history from the University of Notre Dame. She previously headed the museum collections at the Connecticut Historical Society and has edited and authored volumes on George Washington's landscapes, the Alamo, western American art, and Connecticut furniture, tavern signs, and needlework.

MARY V. THOMPSON has served on the staff at Mount Vernon since 1980. Currently the Research Historian, she holds a BA in history, with a minor in folklore, from Samford University in Birmingham, Alabama, and an MA in history from the University of Virginia. She is the author of *In the Hands of a Good Providence: Religion in the Life of George Washington* (2008), for which she received the 2009 Alexandria History Award from the Alexandria Historical Society and the 2013 George Washington Memorial Award from the George Washington Masonic National Memorial.

ESTHER C. WHITE trained as an historical archaeologist, using objects, landscapes, and text to explore people in the past. With interests ranging from public interpretation of history and archaeology at historical sites, museum curatorial issues, and material culture studies, she is the author of articles on diverse subjects, including early American whiskey distilling, the influence of memory on the presentation of sites, and Chesapeake slave life. She holds a BA from the University of North Carolina, an MA from the College of William and Mary, and PhD from the University of Leicester, England. She is the assistant director of the Jefferson Patterson Park and Museum in southern Maryland.

Index

Page numbers in italics refer to illustrations.

Image Credits

Karl Knauer: 16 (bottom), 58
Sara Larson: 58
J. Dean Norton: 29
Edward Owen: back cover (left), 4, 66, 111 (left)
Karen E. Price: 24, 38, 39, 55, 85, 87, 88, 109
Robert Shenk: front cover, ii–iii, 33 (left), 41
Walter Smalling, Jr.: 30, 44
Diana Welsh: 16 (bottom)
Sarah C. Wolfe: 46

Courtesy, American Antiquarian Society: 7 (bottom left), 31 (bottom), 98
Boston Athenæum: 69
The Colonial Williamsburg Foundation: 43 (Gift of Abby Aldrich Rockefeller), 45 (bottom, Museum purchase through the generosity of an Anonymous Donor), 50 (Museum Purchase)
Sally Wern Comport: silhouettes, v, vi, vii, xi, xii, xv, xviii, 7, 8, 10, 15, 19, 20, 27, 30, 34, 37, 40, 42, 44, 49, 52, 56, 59
Fairfax Circuit Court Historic Records: 59
Historical Society of Pennsylvania: 23 (both), 52
Courtesy, Gladys Tancil Holmes, 107 (top), 108
The Huntington Library, San Marino, California: 28, 91 (details)
Courtesy of the John Carter Brown Library at Brown University: 45 (top)
Indianapolis Museum of Art: 54 (Gift of Mrs. M. S. Cassen, 66.63A, imamuseum.org)
Library of Congress, Geography and Map Division, 5, 90; George Washington Papers, 37, 49
Courtesy of the Maryland Historical Society: 7 (top left, detail [1960.108.1.2.21]), 36 [1960.108.1.3.21]
The Metropolitan Museum of Art: 14, 102

©Museo Thyssen-Bornemisza, Madrid: back cover (right), 17 (left)
National Portrait Gallery, Smithsonian Institution: 68
Wynne Patterson: maps, 8, 16, 27, 31, 34, 43, 44, 53
Courtesy, Judge Rohulamin Quander, 106
Virginia Historical Society: 62 (both)
Virginia Museum of Fine Arts, Richmond: 101 (Gift of Edgar William and Bernice Chrysler Garbisch. Photo: Katherine Wetzel)
Yale University Art Gallery: 17 (right, Mabel Brady Garvan Collection, 1946.9.1973. Photo: Gavin Ashworth), 32

Front cover: Farm lane at George Washington's Mount Vernon, on a foggy day in 2014.
Back cover: Left: *Portrait of George Washington,* by Gilbert Stuart, ca. 1798. Right: *Portrait of George Washington's Cook,* attrib. to Gilbert Stuart, 1795–97. Courtesy of the Museo Thyssen-Bornemisza, Madrid.
Endpapers: East Front of Mount Vernon, by Edward Savage, ca. 1787–92.
Pages ii-iii: The memorial erected at Mount Vernon's slave cemetery in 1983 features a truncated granite column, representing "life unfinished." The three steps leading up to the column bear the words, "Faith," "Hope," and "Love," the virtues that sustained those living in bondage.
Frontispiece: First page of a list of enslaved people at Mount Vernon, compiled by George Washington in June 1799.

Lives Bound Together: Slavery at George Washington's Mount Vernon

First Edition, 2016

Published in the United States by
the Mount Vernon Ladies' Association
P.O. Box 110
Mount Vernon, Virginia 22121
www.mountvernon.org

ISBN 978–0–931917–09–7

Book and cover design: Wynne Patterson
Printing: Puritan Capital
Binding: Acme Bookbinding

This book is typeset in Caslon.

Library of Congress Cataloging-in-Publication Data

Names: MacLeod, Jessie, 1986– | Thompson, Mary V., 1955– | Schoelwer, Susan
    Prendergast, editor.
Title: Lives bound together : slavery at George Washington's Mount Vernon /
    introduction by Annette Gordon-Reed ; biographies by Jessie MacLeod ;
    essays by Mary V. Thompson, Philip D. Morgan, Molly H. Kerr, Eleanor
    Breen, Esther C. White, Scott E. Casper, Maurie D. McInnis, Rohulamin
    Quander, Gloria Tancil Holmes, and ZSun-nee Matema ; Susan P. Schoelwer,
    editor.
Description: Mount Vernon, Virginia : Mount Vernon Ladies' Association, 2016.
    | Includes bibliographical references and index.
Identifiers: LCCN 2016030165 | ISBN 9780931917097 (pbk.)
Subjects: LCSH: Washington, George, 1732–1799—Relations with slaves. |
    Slaves—Virginia—Mount Vernon (Estate) | Slavery—Virginia—Mount Vernon
    (Estate) | Mount Vernon (Va. : Estate)—Race relations.
Classification: LCC E312.17 .L78 2016 | DDC 973.4/1092—dc23 LC record
    available at https://lccn.loc.gov/2016030165